THE PROVERBS OF ALFRED

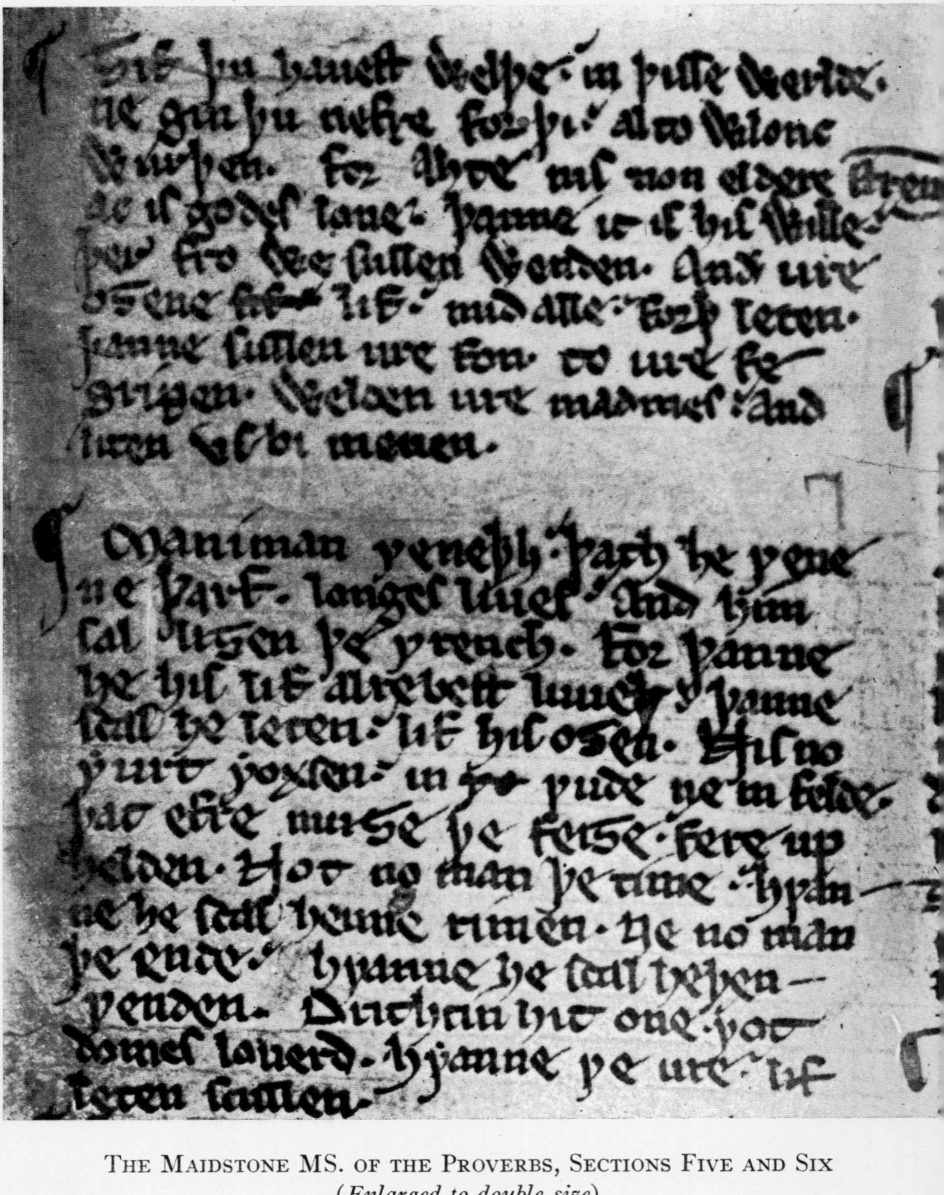

THE MAIDSTONE MS. OF THE PROVERBS, SECTIONS FIVE AND SIX
(*Enlarged to double size*)

THE PROVERBS
OF ALFRED

Studied in the Light of the Recently
Discovered Maidstone Manuscript

by

HELEN PENNOCK SOUTH, PH.D.
Instructor in English, New York University

THE NEW YORK UNIVERSITY PRESS
WASHINGTON SQUARE EAST, NEW YORK CITY
1931

THE NEW YORK UNIVERSITY PRESS

ARTHUR HUNTINGTON NASON, PH.D., DIRECTOR

PRINTED IN THE UNITED STATES OF AMERICA
WAVERLY PRESS, INC.
BALTIMORE, MARYLAND

PREFACE

THE discussion of *The Proverbs of Alfred*, which comprises the larger portion of this volume, was submitted in April, 1929, to the Faculty of Bryn Mawr College as a dissertation in partial fulfillment of the requirements for the degree of Doctor of Philosophy. In publishing this study I have taken the opportunity to provide additional apparatus for the convenience of the reader by appending to the discussion a text and glossary of this important Early Middle English monument. Since the two easily accessible recent editions of the *Proverbs* (Hall, 1920; Skeat, 1907) either print only the unreliable text from Jesus (Oxford) MS. 29, or give it prominence at the expense of other versions, and since neither these editions nor that of Borgström (Lund, 1908) contains the newly discovered Maidstone text, I have felt that a new edition would be of value to scholars. I have, therefore, arranged the texts in such a way as to show in full the readings of the three most reliable versions, and to provide the reader with a composite text which represents the closest possible approach to the archetypal manuscript. A detailed description of my method precedes these texts (pp. 101–2). In the four chapters containing the expository material of this volume, I have endeavored to show the relative value of the extant texts of the *Proverbs*, to present evidence for a twelfth-century date and a Midland locale for the archetype, and to establish the identification of Siford.

To Professor Carleton Brown, whose discovery of the Maidstone MS. of the *Proverbs* supplied the primary impulse for this investigation, I wish to express my deepest gratitude for his inspiration and guidance during the whole course of my research. To me, as to many others, he has revealed the satisfaction and joy to be found in scholarly activity. I also am exceedingly appreciative of the kind assistance that I have received from Dr. Samuel C. Chew and Dr. Howard L. Gray, and from other professors on the Bryn Mawr Faculty.

v

Toward my effort to locate "Siford," Professor Stenton and other members of the Place-name Society of England have generously contributed valuable information. Especially I wish to thank Dr. S. A. Peyton of the University of Reading for the list of Berkshire records that he kindly supplied.

I desire to acknowledge my indebtedness to the staffs of the Bodleian, the Library of Congress, and the libraries of the University of Pennsylvania, New York University, and Bryn Mawr College. To Miss Read and Miss Terrien of Bryn Mawr, whose cheerful co-operation has done much to lighten my work, I feel particularly grateful.

In conclusion, I should like to express my appreciation to Harold C. Whitford, Esq., M.A., of the New York University Press, for editorial and typographical supervision of the publication.

H. P. S.

July, 1931.

CONTENTS

Preface... v

Chapter

    I. Manuscripts and Editions of "The Proverbs of Alfred"   3

   II. The Identification of Siford......................... 25

  III. Early Literary References........................... 43

  IV. The Language of "The Proverbs of Alfred".......... 64

Parallel Text... 99

Glossary... 131

Bibliography... 161

THE PROVERBS OF ALFRED

CHAPTER I

MANUSCRIPTS AND EDITIONS OF "THE PROVERBS OF ALFRED"

THE collection of *Proverbs* associated with the name of King Alfred is preserved, wholly or partially, in three manuscripts: one at Trinity College, Cambridge; one at Jesus College, Oxford; and one in the local museum at Maidstone, Kent.

THE TRINITY MS. (*T.*)

Trinity College Cambridge MS. 323 (shelf-mark B. 14. 39) is described in *The Western Manuscripts in the Library of Trinity College Cambridge: A Descriptive Catalogue by Montague Rhodes James, Litt.D.*, Vol. I (1900), pp. 438–449. No. 323 is a vellum MS. containing a miscellany of religious pieces, both prose and verse, in Latin, French, and English. Dr. James's list of the contents includes forty-three articles. Between 1863 and 1896 this MS. was missing from the Trinity College Library, having been accidentally packed in a box belonging to a Fellow of the College, which remained unopened until his death.[1] The MS. has frequently been stated to be of the first half of the thirteenth century;[2] but, inasmuch as it contains on fol. 83 a Latin epitaph on Robert Grosseteste, Bishop of Lincoln, the later leaves (including the *Proverbs*) cannot have been written before October, 1253. The pieces in MS. 323 have been written by a number of hands. This fact would indicate that the book belonged to a religious house, and that members of the convent entered material in it for the common use.

The Proverbs of Alfred is written on fols. 85–87 in double columns of 35 lines. Immediately preceding (in a different hand) are short pieces in Latin verse on the "Three Sorrowful Things," etc. Following the *Proverbs* on the verso of fol. 87 are also Latin verses con-

---

[1] For an account of the recovery and return of this MS. to the Library, see the letter of W. Aldis Wright in *The [Lon-* *don] Times*, July 13, 1896.
[2] Skeat, *The Proverbs of Alfred*, p. vii.

taining definitions of love, etc.   The hand that copied the *Proverbs* is, according to Dr. James, similar to that of the long Biblical poem on fol. 36 ff.   After examining the rotograph of the manuscript, I have come to the conclusion that the hands are identical.   The general appearance of the handwriting is similar, and in both pieces a paragraph mark of unusual form occurs.   The individual letters correspond closely; variations, as for example two forms of *r*, may be found in both poems.   Each contains the long *s* and the round *s*.   The curious crossed *w* of the Biblical poem also appears in the *Proverbs*, although not so frequently.   The only letter which is peculiar to the *Proverbs* is ȝ, which in form somewhat resembles the figure *5*.   The presence of this symbol, which I have not noted elsewhere in the MS., may be explained by its probable occurrence in the copy used by the scribe in writing the *Proverbs*.

The plummet-writing at the bottom of the folios on which the Biblical poem is written is probably also by the same scribe, although, on account of the use of the plummet, its appearance is much more stiff than that of the other two poems.   This plummet-writing, which has been partially erased, was an earlier draft of the Epiphany song, later copied in ink, which begins: "Wolle ye iheren of twelte day."

The text of the *Proverbs* in the Trinity MS. shows frequent confusion of þ and ƿ and of *w* and ȝ.   Professor Skeat would explain this by supposing that the scribe was a Norman who was not familiar with these peculiar English characters.[3]   He finds further indication in the occurrence at the bottom of fol. 85a of a row of English characters with the name of each inscribed above:

iȝe	w	ant	iþorn
ȝ	ƿ	7	þ

It is interesting to observe that a similar row of characters with the designation of each appears in the Maidstone MS. of the *Proverbs*, which will be discussed below.

The Jesus MS. (*J.*)

Jesus College Oxford MS. 29 consists of (Part I) a parchment MS. written in the fifteenth century and (Part II) a vellum MS. of

[3] *Op. cit.*, p. xiv ff.

the thirteenth, now bound together. It has been described by H. O. Coxe, *Catalogus Codicum MSS. qui in Collegiis Aulisque Oxoniensibus hodie adservantur*, Pars II, 1852. The thirteenth-century section, from fol. 144 (or fol. 217 according to the pagination in ink) to the end of the book, was written by a single hand. Mr. E. W. B. Nicholson, sometime Bodley's librarian, contributed the following information concerning the date of this portion of the MS.:

"From f. 217 [i.e., fol. 144] to the end of the volume is apparently all in one hand, and was certainly written about the same time. It contains a history of Tobias which mentions the then Prior of St. Mary Kenilworth (Gwilleyme); this fixes the date of *composition* at 1276–9, and I believe that to be approximately the date of the writing."[4]

The Jesus MS. contains, besides *The Proverbs of Alfred* (fol. 262 ff.), a considerable number of moral and religious poems in Middle English (printed by Morris in *E.E.T.S.*, orig. ser. XLIX) and also a text of *The Owl and the Nightingale*.

THE MAIDSTONE MS. (*M.*)

For an account of Manuscript A. 13 in the Museum at Maidstone, Kent, the reader should consult Carleton Brown, "A Thirteenth-Century Manuscript at Maidstone" (*Modern Language Review*, XXI (1926), 1–12). The date of this MS., in the opinion of Mr. J. A. Herbert of the British Museum, can hardly be later than 1250. The MS. contains a fragmentary text (11 stanzas) of the Old French poem, *Les Vers de la Mort*, composed by Bishop Helinand between 1194 and 1197,[5] and an Anglo-Norman orison to the Blessed Virgin in five ten-line stanzas. The only Middle English material in the MS. aside from the *Proverbs* is a text of the poem warning against death, which begins "Man mei longe him liues wene," (on the verso of the leaf containing the *Proverbs*), and six lines of verse on the Three Sorrowful Tidings (fol. 243b) introduced into a Latin prose treatise. With these exceptions the contents of the Maidstone MS. are entirely in Latin. A considerable number

---

[4] As quoted by Miss Anna Paues, *Anglia*, XXX (1907), 222.

[5] *Mod. Lang. Rev.*, XXI, 4–6; cf. also pp. 259–60.

of hands appear in the book, all of them apparently of the thirteenth
century.   This manuscript, like that in the Trinity Library, evidently was compiled in some religious house.   Professor Brown suc-
ceeded in identifying the house to which the book belonged as the
Cluniac Priory of St. Andrew at Northampton.   As evidence he
points to the appearance of a Latin prayer to St. Andrew on fol.
221a appended to a series of prayers to Christ and the Virgin, and to
the occurrence of numerous Northamptonshire place-names and personal names in an itemized record of local expenses entered on fols.
6b and 7a in space which had been left vacant on these pages.   The
entry of these accounts must belong to a distinctly later date than
the other material in the volume; but by identifying several of the
persons named, Professor Brown fixed the time at which the accounts were added as *circa* 1300.

On the top margin of fol. 93a, immediately above the text of the
Proverbs, and written apparently by the same hand, is the following
series of Middle English characters, together with their respective
names:[6]

þorn	andt	iye	wen	þath	yod
þ	7	ʒ	ꝥ	ꝥ	1

This series presents interesting similarities to the one already described in the Trinity College MS.; and, in both cases, it is to be
noted, this row of characters occurs in connection with a text of
the *Proverbs*.   So far as I am aware, the only other case of the sort
is found in McClean MS. 123, in the Fitzwilliam Museum, Cambridge, a manuscript of about 1300.   In the McClean MS. as
described by Miss Anna Paues (*Anglia*, XXX, 218), the symbols
listed are þ ꝥ ʒ 1.   The list is written on the verso of fol. 114, thus
facing the text of the Middle English *Poema Morale*, which begins
on fol. 115a.   The contents of the McClean MS. down to fol. 114
are entirely in French.   Skeat, discussing the Trinity MS. of the
Proverbs, suggested that "before the scribe began to write out the
poem, he made a note of four new characters which he had to
employ."   This explanation, however, leaves out of account the

[6] The MS. has been trimmed at the top,   culty in distinguishing the names of the
a fact which causes the reader some diffi-   symbols.

apparent identity of the hand which appears in the *Proverbs* and in
the English plummet-writing. Moreover, if the scribe were setting
down these characters for his own guidance, he would hardly have
written them at the bottom of the page. It may be conceded that
in all three MSS. these English characters were named for the
benefit of persons unfamiliar with English, but it would seem quite
as probable that they were set down for the convenience of the
reader as for that of the scribe.

The *Proverbs* are copied in the Maidstone MS. on fol. 93a in three
columns in a compact hand, with the heading "Dicta Alfredi."
Unfortunately the Maidstone MS. gives us selections from the
Proverbs instead of a complete text. These selections comprise
266 lines, the first three and the last nine sections of the poem
being omitted as well as some intermediate parts. Several interesting scribal peculiarities are exhibited. In the first five sections the scribe writes *w*, but afterwards changes to *p*.[7] At least
six examples of the use of *w* for *ȝ* suggest that his original contained
p in all sections, and that the scribe, being unfamiliar with *p* and *ȝ*,
confused these two characters. After the scribe had copied half of
the third section, he apparently became aware of his error and thereafter wrote *ȝ* accurately, but in the form of a French *g*. No examples
of the use of *þ* occur, and *7* is used infrequently. The scribe pre-
fers to spell out *7* as well as *þ*, although the list of symbols at the
head of the text contains both characters. Several erasures in this
series suggest that the scribe was not entirely familiar with these
symbols.

THE COTTON MS.

Cotton Galba A. XIX is not extant. This manuscript was
either the archetype of the *Proverbs*, or very close to it. Wanley,
the most authoritative paleographer of the early eighteenth century, who actually saw the MS. before its destruction by fire in
1731, says in his catalogue of Anglo-Saxon MSS. appended as a
third volume to Hickes's *Thesaurus*,[8] that it was in a fragmentary
condition at that time (1705). He continues his description:

[7] By referring to the frontispiece facsimile,   [8] P. 231.
the reader may observe the two forms.

". . . litteris Normanno-Saxonicis circa temp. Henrici II. aut Ricardi I. conscriptum in quo continentur quædam ex Proverbiis et Apophthegmatis Ælfredi Regis sapientissimi." Fortunately three transcripts of this manuscript were made, but none of them is complete.

THE WANLEY TRANSCRIPT (*W.*)

The Wanley transcript is a direct copy of the first thirty lines, printed by Wanley together with his description of the manuscript. It is the most valuable of the transcripts because it is the only one made from the MS. without an intermediate copy. Several Old English characters are used, and the text as far as it is possible to judge by comparison with the other transcripts shows a high degree of accuracy.

THE SPELMAN TRANSCRIPT (*Sp.*)

The Spelman transcript, which contains only the first 95 lines, was made some time previous to 1643, the date of Sir John Spelman's death. It was taken from a copy made by Sir Thomas Cotton himself,[9] according to Spelman, who introduces it into his *Life of Alfred the Great* by the following remarks:[10]

. . . as they [*Proverbs*] are I cannot think it fit to offer them unto the World, as an Instance of what the King composed. For they are not his very Work in the Saxon Tongue, but a Miscellany Collection of some later Author, who, according to his own Faculty, hath in a broken English put together such of the sayings of King Ælfred, as he met withal, some of them Rimeing, and others (as perhaps the Original was) in Prose: and besides that in their Order they somewhat argue the Collector's want of Judgment. For marshalling them no better, the copy is so faulty and ill writ, in a mungrel Hand, (as well as Language) as that unless I should, without Regard, venture to trespass against the Truth, I dare not publish it according to the Copy I have taken. Therefore whereas there are 31 Heads of the Sayings of the King, all beginning with

[9] Sir Robert Bruce Cotton died in 1631, and his MSS. became the property of his son Thomas. Skeat suggests (p. xxiv, n. 2) that the Cotton transcript used by Spelman was probably made after this transfer, which would date the lost manuscript 1631–43.

[10] *Life of Alfred the Great*, 1709, pp. 125–26.

these words, *Thus quoth Ælfred*, I take them not all, onely the Beginning of them, and three or four of the first only (which are the perfectest) I have (to shew the Style and Manner of them) set down, in the words that I have copied them, together with the current Sense they have in Speech at this Day. For the Residue I have taken such as I presume I read right and understand, and I have only set them down in English, noting them with Figures, according to the number or place they hold among the rest.

It is greatly to be regretted that Sir John felt such scruples about presenting the text exactly as he had it before him. However, his note on the number of sections and the paraphrase of certain portions has been of value in reconstructing the order and content of the original manuscript.

Spelman's *Life of Alfred the Great* is found in three forms: MS. Rawlinson D. 324, which is Thomas Hearne's transcript as prepared for the press; the *Life* of 1709, printed with minor variations from Rawlinson; and a translation into Latin by Christopher Wase, published with a commentary by Obadiah Walker in 1678.[11] The Rawlinson version, as the closest to the original, is the preferable, although the least accessible text.

THE JAMES TRANSCRIPT (*Jms.*)

Richard James (1592–1638), librarian for Sir Robert Bruce Cotton and also for his son, Sir Thomas, transcribed extracts amounting to about 119 lines from a copy supplied by Mr. Thomas Allen, according to a note at the end of the manuscript, now James 6, Bodleian Library.[12] This MS., known to Kemble, was called to Skeat's attention by Professor W. Heuser of Göttingen.[13] Skeat then tried to identify the Allen copy on which James was based. This he thought was Digby 4, which now contains no Alfredian proverbs, but was catalogued in 1696 by Bernard as containing "Alfredi Regis Parabolæ Saxonice."[14] The question as to whether this manuscript, which was among those bequeathed by Thomas

---

[11] *Dict. of Nat. Biog.*, XVIII, 742. A fragmentary copy of this translation is preserved in Stowe MS. 163, Art. 18.

[12] The James text is printed in full by Professor Brown in *Mod. Lang. Rev.*, XXI (1926), 256–57.

[13] Skeat, *op. cit.*, p. xxiii.

[14] Bernard's *Catalogue* of 1696, p. 68.

Allen at his death in 1633 to Sir Kenelm Digby, ever did contain Alfredian "Parabolæ," is one of great interest. Joseph Hall has indicated the right answer by pointing out the false identification of the *Poema Morale* with *The Proverbs of Alfred* made by Langbaine.[15] He also calls attention to an earlier instance of the same mistake, showing that Digby 4 MS. never did contain "Alfredi Regis Parabolæ." "This is clear," he says, "from MS. Rawlinson D. 325, which consists of Hearne's notes to Spelman's *Life of Alfred;* it contains the note printed on page 131 of the *Life*, which is immediately followed by a *cancelled* extract from the *Poema Morale* in the Digby version." The Spelman note reads: "Amongst Sir Kenelm Digby's MSS. (num. iv) in the Bodlejan Library is another Tract, call'd *Alfred's Proverbs;* which, however, is of a late date, and contains certain Rhapsodies about the different Conditions of Man's Life. The learned Dr. Hicks has printed some part of it in his *Thesaurus, Lingg. Sept.*, p. 222, to whom I refer you for a further Account of it. . . ." On turning to Hickes's *Thesaurus*, we find selections from the *Poema Morale*.[16]

Whereas Spelman rewrote the "semi-barbarous" language of his text before presenting it to the public, James apparently has given us a fairly accurate copy. A number of Old English characters are consistently used, as was the case in the Cotton MS. according to Wanley. That the Cotton MS. was the original of the James

---

[15] J. Hall, *Selections from Early Middle English*, II, 286. Reference to Folio Catalogue of Bodleian MSS., col. 5, note 1, gives an additional point of proof. Here E. W. B. Nicholson, then Bodleian librarian, states that at the end of the description of Digby 4 in Langbaine's autograph (Cod. Langbaine XIX, p. 455), the words *non comparent* are added to "Alfredi Regis Parabolæ, Saxonice"; and that Langbaine's index, made about 1650, contains no mention of the "Parabolæ." These facts seem to indicate that Langbaine, perhaps misled by the similarity in didactic tone and use of the first person, and probably knowing that James had used an Allen MS., had originally identified all or part of the *Poema Morale* of that MS. with "Alfredi Regis Parabolæ," but later, in verifying his list, had corrected the mistake. Bernard, however, evidently failed to note the correction.

[16] Hickes heads his chapter, "De Poetica Semi-Saxonica, sive corrupta poesi Anglo-Saxonum," and after some discussion of changes in the language, gives selected stanzas of the *Poema Morale* as his first illustration. Since he mentions the Trinity and Lambeth texts and collates them with his Digby extracts, he evidently knew the *Poema Morale* thoroughly and did not share Spelman's misapprehension.

transcript (the MS. from which the Allen copy was made) is supposed because James corresponds closely to Wanley, the only direct copy, and because Hearne collated James with the Spelman text when he prepared it for the press (Rawlinson D. 324). This procedure shows that he believed the James transcript originated from the same source as Spelman's.

From the evidence afforded by these three transcripts, one short but direct, the other two longer but second-hand, we may draw the following conclusions about the original Cotton MS. First, it contained a number of Old English characters; second, it was composed of at least 31 sections not counting the introduction (32 altogether), as shown by Spelman's account of its condition at the time when the Thomas Cotton copy was lent to him. This conclusion is corroborated by the lines at the end of the James transcript which correspond to a portion of section 32 in the Trinity MS. Third, that the first 30 lines were, with some very slight variations, the same as Wanley's copy; and fourth, that James, whose high degree of accuracy is attested by the close agreement existing between his copy and Wanley's, may be trusted to give a fairly dependable idea of nearly 90 additional lines. The less accurate Spelman version of the first 95 lines, together with his paraphrase, is of value in checking up the work of James and Wanley, but is to be used with caution when unsupported.

EDITIONS

The Trinity and Jesus MSS. were the first to be made accessible to the public. These appeared in the *Reliquiæ Antiquæ*, the collection of pieces from early manuscripts edited by Thomas Wright and James Orchard Halliwell, London, 1841.[17] This is primarily an edition of the Trinity text. Mention is made of the Cotton MS. and its fate, and two of the transcripts are noted, but no variant readings are offered. The Jesus MS., however, is given in full at the foot of the pages. It is printed, according to Wright, from a transcript by Sir Frederic Madden. The Trinity text of this edition is very unreliable, but the Jesus version is much more correct, as might be expected, since the manuscript is less difficult

[17] I, 170–88.

to read than that of Trinity.   The edition has no notes or glossary.

The second publication of the *Proverbs* was that by John M. Kemble in the appendix (pp. 225–57) of his edition of *The Dialogue of Salomon and Saturnus*, printed for the Ælfric Society in 1848. Kemble used the Trinity text, perhaps from his own transcript.[18] His edition contains a great number of mistakes, some of which were handed down from Wright.[19]   Kemble gives no readings from other texts, but mentions the Cotton MS. and its transcripts, and also speaks of a MS. in Lincoln College, Oxford, a reference which is now believed to have been an error for Jesus College, since he does not refer to the Jesus text elsewhere.   Although the text of only one manuscript is given, Kemble's discussion of this poem is of value; for he includes a number of parallels to the *Proverbs* from other literature, both English and Continental.   He also accompanies his text with "a rough translation, without which," he says, "it would be scarcely intelligible."

The Proverbs of Alfred was published for the third time by Richard Morris, in his *Old English Miscellany*,[20] with the text of the Jesus MS. and of the Trinity MS. arranged on facing pages.   In order to parallel the two texts, he changed the order of *T*. to match that of *J*., and numbered the lines according to *J*.   He even counted lines missing in *T*. and found in *J*., so that the sum total of lines ascribed to *T*. is greater than the actual number.   The Jesus text is printed accurately as a result of correcting Wright's text by the actual manuscript.   Skeat, who compared Morris's edition of Jesus with the MS., reports no errors.[21]   The Trinity text is still unreliable, but this could hardly be otherwise, since the MS. was lost at that time.   Morris was therefore obliged to compile his own text from a comparison of the Wright and Kemble editions.   He was able to correct some errors, but naturally fell into others, since the original could only be conjectured.   Morris makes no mention of the Cotton MS. or its transcripts, nor does he give other notes. He does, however, print a glossary for his volume, which is helpful, although not complete.[22]

[18] Skeat, *op. cit.*, p. ix.
[19] For list of mistakes of both Wright and Kemble, see Borgström, *The Proverbs of Alfred*, Lund, 1908, pp. vi–ix.

[20] *E.E.T.S.*, orig. ser., XLIX (1872), 102–38.
[21] Skeat, *op. cit.*, p. x.
[22] Morris printed some extracts from the

A fourth edition of the *Proverbs* was made in 1907 by the Reverend Walter W. Skeat, published at the Clarendon Press, Oxford. In his preface he says: "My chief object in publishing a new edition of *The Proverbs of Alfred* is to give for the first time a correct text of the more important and longer text contained in the Trin. Coll. Camb. MS., which has hitherto been very incorrectly reproduced, though it has already been issued three times." After such a profession, it seems odd that Skeat should give so much more prominence to the Jesus MS. He prints this on the left-hand page with Trinity on the right, and dislocates the latter to make it fit *J.*, in spite of his previous criticism of Morris for the same arrangement.[23] Thus the promised correct text of Trinity appears in an order different from that in the manuscript.[24] Moreover, Skeat prints a restored text, although the MS. reading is given in the footnotes. He explains his purpose in these words (p. xxvii): "As this text [*T.*] abounds with errors of spelling of many kinds, it was considered advisable to restore it throughout, so as to show the forms which the scribe, in all probability, had before him. All such corrections are accounted for in the footnotes."

At the bottom of the pages for comparison with the Trinity and Jesus MSS., Skeat also prints a third text of 98 lines, compiled from the transcripts of the Cotton Galba MS. As the James transcript is the only one which exceeds that length, Skeat does not print it as a whole, but indicates in the notes where it differs from the Trinity text. Skeat's edition also contains explanatory notes with sources and parallels for the *Proverbs*, a discussion of the grammar and metre of the poem, and a glossary.

In 1908, a fifth edition of *The Proverbs of Alfred* was published at Lund. It was edited by Edv. Borgström, who as early as 1900 had submitted his text of the Trinity MS.[25] to the Philosophical Faculty of the University of Lund as part of the treatise for his

Jesus MS. with a few notes in his *Specimens of Early English*, Part I, Oxford, 1882. A revised edition of this was made by Skeat in 1885.

[23] *Trans. of the Phil. Soc.* (1895–98), 402.

[24] Skeat gives the correct numbering of the lines at the head of each section, but uses numbers in the margin which correspond to the order of *J.*

[25] Borgström, *The Proverbs of Alfred*, Preface.

Licentiate Examination. Since the Trinity MS. had been re-covered in 1896, there was great need of a new and accurate edition of the text. Mr. Borgström, however, was delayed in writing the other portions of his treatise on account of teaching duties, but had part of it in press when Skeat's edition came out. Since Borgström was presenting not only texts and glossary, but valuable notes, especially on the phonology, grammar, and metrics of the poem, he continued with his plans for publication in spite of the appearance of Skeat's text.

In several respects his edition is superior to Skeat's. In the first place, he does not try to print the Trinity and Jesus MSS. in parallel form, and so the true order is kept intact. Secondly, he prints the manuscript reading unless it is unintelligible, in which case he gives it in the notes. This method affords a much better idea of the original than is to be gained from Skeat's more freely edited text. In the third place, the notes on the language of the poem are much more extensive than those of Skeat.

Borgström prints first the Trinity text, as the more important, and then the Jesus version. After that he gives Spelman's tran-script, with variants from Wanley. The James transcript he does not know except through Skeat's readings.

The combined work of Skeat and Borgström seemed to render a new text of the *Proverbs* unnecessary; and doubtless no sixth edition would have appeared, had not Joseph Hall wished to include the Jesus redaction in his *Selections from Early Middle English*, Oxford, 1920.[26] In contrast to other editors, he prints this text in long lines, in an effort to show its similarity to Anglo-Saxon verse. Although the reprinting of the Jesus MS. is not of so much value to those who have access to the former editions, yet no one can regret it, since it afforded Mr. Hall the opportunity to print some valuable notes on the poem.[27]

---

[26] I, 18–28.

[27] *Ibid.*, II, 285–308. Other discussions of *The Proverbs of Alfred* are: Wülcker, "Über die Neu-Angelsächsischen Sprüche des Königs Ælfred," Paul and Braune's *Beiträge*, I (1874), 240 ff.; E. Gropp, *The Proverbs of Alfred*, Halle, 1879, (a disser-tation); Skeat, "The Proverbs of Alfred," *Transactions of the Philological Society*, (1895–98), 399–418. See also J. Schip-per, *Englische Metrik*, Bonn, 1881.

The Relative Value of the Manuscripts

It is unfortunate that editors have given so much prominence to the Jesus manuscript, which is, after all, the latest of the group. The characteristics of the archetype have been conjectured largely from the peculiarities of this one text, the least reliable of the versions, as I shall try to show. In the remainder of the chapter, I shall compare the manuscripts with regard to the order of the sections, the omission or addition of lines, and clear readings as against obviously corrupted passages. In this way, some conclusion may be reached as to the fidelity of each MS. to the lost original.

Order of Sections

The Cotton MS. contained at least 31 sections plus an introduction, according to Spelman, who also gave us a good idea of its order through his quotation and paraphrase. His outline is supported by the James transcript. Although the latter is a series of extracts, each is in its proper place as indicated in the Spelman résumé.

The same arrangement is found in the Trinity MS., although here there are 37 sections. This number perhaps represents the original length of the Cotton Galba text, the last leaf of which may have been lost before Sir Thomas Cotton made the copy that he lent to Spelman. Leaves so frequently slough off that unique material at the end of one version more often means better preservation of the original than a late addition.

The new Maidstone MS., although a series of selections similar to the James transcript, supports this Cotton-Trinity order with the exception of the transposition of section 28 and the two lines from section 16, (numbered according to *T.*).

The Jesus MS., on the other hand, shows great variation from the original order so well attested by the agreement of the other manuscripts. This fact will be thoroughly impressed upon any one who works with parallel passages in the various versions. It is one great obstacle to Skeat's assumption (p. xii) that *J.* lies nearer to the original than the other manuscripts. Further objections will appear later.

Omission or Addition of Lines

The Cotton transcripts and the Maidstone MS., although not complete, contain no lines not vouched for by one or more other manuscripts.[28] They are thus very valuable as far as they go.

Each of the two longer versions, Trinity (668 lines) and Jesus (456 lines), contains material not found in the other, or in Maidstone or the transcripts. Skeat, whose enthusiasm is not shared by all scholars, says (p. xii) in regard to them: "Text A [designation for Jesus MS. in his edition] is considerably shorter than Text B [Trinity], and there seems to be no reason why we may not regard it as representing (in a somewhat late copy) the earlier text of the two."

In spite of Skeat's assertion, several reasons may be advanced against accepting the Jesus MS. as closer to the original than Trinity. When two texts of differing lengths are compared in an effort to decide their proximity to the archetype, it is never safe to conclude that the longer is a later, expanded form. A scribe of creative ability, making a copy for his own pleasure or for some particular purpose, often exercised the editorial art of condensation and selection. On the other hand, he might also expand the text at some point where he fancied explanation or emphasis was needed, a method which may account for several places where the Jesus text contains lines not found elsewhere.

The Jesus MS. omits 256 lines that appear in Trinity. Of these, 127 lines are supported by one or more of the other MSS. (Maidstone, James, or Spelman paraphrase).[29] This fact indicates that the Jesus text is not a complete reproduction of the original. Moreover, the lines found in the Jesus MS., and not in Trinity, are only in one case (*J.* 37–8) supported by other readings. Here James and Spelman support:

> Mildeliche ich munye,
> myne leoue freond,

---

[28] An unimportant exception may be found in *Sp.* 71,* where Spelman inserted *engle frofre* as in the preceding section.

[29] Trinity, lines 191, 245–63, 297–315, 365–383, 403–421, 435–6, 462–501, 532–668. Of these, Maidstone supports 246–63, 298–315, 463–84, 486–501; James, 404–421, 611–12; Spelman paraphrase, 485–501, 532–564. References to Trinity are designated by Borgström's numbering. I have retained Skeat's numbering for all passages from the Jesus MS.

lines which were probably omitted carelessly by the Trinity scribe. The unsupported lines are pretty clearly expansions, such as 80–1. The preceding lines read:

> And þe clerk and þe knyht
> schulle démen euenliche riht;

> ll. 80–1   þe poure and þe ryche
> [hi schulle] démen ilyche.

This couplet is obviously an expansion of *euenliche*, and is not even complete.

In addition to these lines, section six in Jesus is not found in Trinity, James, Spelman, or Maidstone. Borgström complains that this paragraph on the profit of acquiring knowledge in youth, breaks the continuity.[30] This is certainly the case, for the preceding section has described the knight's duty of protecting the churl so that the latter may be in peace to sow his seed, mow his mead, and drive his ploughs; and the next section according to Trinity, reminds the reader that seventy acres and other wealth are of no value without wisdom. Apparently the Jesus scribe, or some predecessor, after copying the part about the peaceful cultivation of land, looked ahead and saw that wisdom was mentioned in the next paragraph. This perhaps reminded him of Alfred's words on wisdom and his desire that learning should be cultivated among the young, as expressed in the preface to the *Pastoral Care*.[31] Feeling that this matter might be appropriately introduced at this point, he inserted a section on the subject before returning to the connection between husbandry and wisdom.

J. 290–91 are unimportant and may be regarded as a dull expansion of the preceding thought. *J*. 337–8 are also an expansion, but lines 333–34 represent the insertion of a common saying, which apparently struck the writer as appropriate to the subject:

> For hit seyþ in þe l[e]oþ,
> 'as scumes, forteoþ.'

---

[30] Borgström, *op. cit.*, p. xv.

[31] ". . . ðætte eall sīo gioguð ðe nū is on Angelcynne frīora monna, ðāra ðe ðā spēda hæbben ðæt hīe ðæm befeolan mægen, sīen tō liornunga oðfæste, ðā hwīle ðe hīe tō nānre ōðerre note ne mægen, oð ðone first ðe hīe wel cunnen Englisc gewrit ārædan: lære mon siððan furður on Lædengeðīode ðā ðe mon furðor læran wille, ond tō hīerran hāde dōn wille."

J. 369–70 give a common didactic reflection; and the tendency to insert commonplaces of a suitable proverbial nature is also shown in section 23. In order to show the havoc wrought in the latter part of this paragraph by the scribe of Jesus or his predecessor, I shall give the three extant texts in parallel columns before discussing them. The Maidstone MS. is of great value here in proving the authenticity of the Trinity version.

TRINITY	MAIDSTONE	JESUS
þis child is fadiris blisse.	Þis child is fader blisse	Wis child is fader blisse.
ʒif it so bitidit,	if it so bitideþ	If hit so bi-tydeþ
þad þu chil ƿeldest,	þat tu bern ƿeldest	þat þu bern ibidest,
þe ƿile þat hit is litil,	hƿiles it his litel	þe hwile hit is lutel
þu lere him monnis þeƿis;	ler hit mannes þeƿes	ler him mon-þewes.
þanne hit is ƿoxin,	þanne it is ƿoxen	þanne hit is wexynde,
he sal ƿenne þer-to;	it scal ƿenden þer-to	hit schal wende þar-to;
þanne sal þe child	þanne scal þi bern	þe betere hit schal iwurþe
þas þe bet þurþen.	þas þe beth þurþen	euer buuen eorþe.
ac ʒif þu lef him ƿel-den	7 if þu letest him ƿel-den	Ac if þu him lest welde,
al his oƿene ƿille,	al ƿille his oʒen	wexende on worlde,
		lude and stille,
		his owene wille,
þanne he comit to helde,	þanne he cumeþ to elde	hwanne cumeþ ealde,
sore it sal him reƿen,	sore it scal him reƿen	ne myht þu hyne awelde;
7 he sal banne þat ƿidt	7 me scal banne þe ƿit	þanne deþ hit sone
þat him first taʒte;	þat him furst tahte;	þat þe biþ vnyqueme,
þanne sal þi child	þanne scal þi bern	ofer-howeþ þin ibod,
þi forbod ouer-gan-gin.	þi bode ouergangen	and makeþ þe ofte sory-mod.
beter þe ƿere	betere þe ƿere	Betere þe were
child þat þu ne haue-dest;	bern þat tu nahtest	iboren þat he nere;

TRINITY	MAIDSTONE	JESUS
for betere is child vnboren	for betere is bern un-born	for betere is child vn-bore
þenne vnbeten.	þanne unibeten.	þane vnbuhsum.
		þe mon þe spareþ yeorde
		and yonge childe,
		and let hit arixlye
		þat he hit areche ne may,
		þat him schal on ealde sore reowe. Amen.

All three manuscripts agree fairly closely for the first ten lines; then *J.* inserts the trite expressions:

> wexende on worlde,
> lude and stille.

Perhaps the *J.* scribe could not resist the opportunity to make a rime with *wille* in the next line.   The combination of *lude and stille* with a line ending in *wille* is very common in Layamon's *Brut*, and also in *The Owl and the Nightingale*, which the Jesus scribe copied. It is also to be found elsewhere in the *Proverbs*, (*T.* 429 and *J.* 325).   The Jesus scribe then continues paraphrasing loosely for another ten lines, after which he adds several of his own and concludes with a sentence found in *T.* and *M.* in an entirely different position, (*T.* 235–36, *M.* 235–36).   The new material, it should be noted, is only an expansion of the Biblical motto, "Spare the rod and spoil the child."[32]   The most interesting lines in this section are those given by *T.* as,

> for betere is child vnboren
> þenne vnbeten.

These are closely supported by *M.*, although the word *bern* is used for *child.   J.*, however, spoils the force of the passage by reading *vnbuhsum* (disobedient) for *vnbeten*.   That this reading is not

---

[32] *Proverbs* XIII, 24: "He that spareth his rod, hateth his son: but he that loveth   him, chasteneth him betimes."

only wrong from the standpoint of literary feeling, but also from the point of view of the texts, is proved by the use of *unibeten* in Maidstone and *non castigari* in Spelman's Latin paraphrase.[33]

There is, therefore, no reason why the Trinity MS. should fall in the reader's esteem because of the lack of some lines found only in Jesus. With the exception of the two lines (*J*. 37–8), which are supported by other manuscripts, the unique passages of *J*. may be suspected as scribal elaborations. Let us consider, then, the lines which are peculiar to Trinity, to see if these, too, may be attributed to a scribe. It has already been noted that of the 256 lines of Trinity not found in Jesus, 127 are vouched for by other manuscripts. This leaves 129, of which 104 occur after the close of the Spelman paraphrase (which corresponds to l. 564 of *T*.). The possibility that a leaf was lost at the close of the Cotton text has already been suggested. This conjecture is supported by two lines quoted by James, (*T*. 611–12). Although it cannot be fully proved, the chance that these hundred lines represent the end of the archetypal MS. seems greater than that they are a scribal elaboration.

This leaves *T*. 191, 365–383, 435–6, if "þus quad alured" be omitted, which is used only once in James and not at all in Maidstone. *T*. 191, "wines mine," occurs in a section only given elsewhere in *J*. It is more in accordance with the usual scribal mistakes to suppose that the *J*. scribe carelessly omitted this unessential vocative in copying, rather than that the *T*. scribe inserted it. Section 22 in *T*. (lines 365–383) and lines 435–6 fit into the content of the poem and offer no evidence of later insertion.

In subject-matter, then, as well as in order, the Cotton transcripts, the Maidstone MS., and Trinity unite to give us the original MS. tradition against Jesus, which in a number of cases shows signs of extensive rearrangement and editing.

CORRECT READINGS

The correct reading may usually be established by an agreement among the manuscripts. The Cotton transcripts, although incomplete, are most valuable in the support that they afford. They are

---

[33] Noted by Professor Brown, *Mod. Lang.* *Rev.*, XXI (July, 1926), 258. The *Life* of 1709 reads *unbeaten*.

particularly helpful in providing a criterion for Trinity passages, which are sometimes marred by scribal misspellings and other errors. In cases where the Jesus MS. gives a better reading than Trinity, it will be found that Trinity is not supported by the other MSS. When it is so supported, it is more reliable than Jesus, whose scribe is given to paraphrasing and occasional personal interpretation. An illustration of this has already been given in the section quoted in regard to rearing a child, where, among other divergencies, *J.* uses *vnbuhsum* for *vnbeten*, although the agreement between Trinity, Maidstone, and the Spelman paraphrase proves it incorrect.

The discovery of the Maidstone text has been of great value in establishing good readings. In some cases its support has lent the needed authority either to Trinity or Jesus in a disputed passage.[34] Again it has given wording entirely different from any other version, but so intelligible that there could be no doubt as to its truth. Among the examples noted by Professor Brown, is the use of the Old English word *wræcsið*, (*M.* 120, *wrakesih*), otherwise unknown in Middle English.[35] The scribe of *T.* made two words of it, *wrake se*, but *J.* gave it up and substituted an entirely different word, *wowe.*

EVIDENCES OF AGE

In addition to conformity to the manuscript traditions of order, content, and wording, an individual MS. may be judged, at least to some extent, by its claims to priority. Of course it is possible for a later copy to reproduce the archetype more faithfully than an earlier one, but in general the older text may be considered the more valuable, unless divergencies or serious inaccuracies can be proved against it.

The paleography of Jesus 29, and Mr. Nicholson's evidence for its date, mentioned above, indicate that it is the latest of the versions. The Trinity MS., or at least the leaves containing the *Proverbs*, cannot be earlier than 1253.

The Maidstone MS., as has been stated on the authority of J. A.

---

[34] For examples, see "The Maidstone Text of *The Proverbs of Alfred*," *Mod.* *Lang. Rev.*, XXI (July, 1926), 258.
[35] *Ibid.*, p. 259.

Herbert of the British Museum, is not later than 1250. That it is much earlier seems probable on account of the archaisms. *Wrakesih* (O.E.—*wræcsið*) has already been noted. We also find *maþeleþ* (O.E.—*maðelian*) in line 312. This was not understood by *T.*, who wrote *mamelit*. Moreover, the fact that *M.* at times agrees with *T.* or *J.* as against the other, shows that it belongs to the parent stem previous to the forking of *T.* and *J.* Professor Carleton Brown points out further evidence in line 117.[36] Here Trinity reads: "for god may ʒiuen." *J.* also uses *god*, but Maidstone reads *crist*. That this was the original form is proved by Spelman's Latin paraphrase, which gives *Christus*. This example again shows that the MS. from which *M.* was copied preceded both *T.* and *J.* in the direct line of descent.

The use of some of the Old English symbols also deserves notice. According to Wanley, the Cotton Galba MS. was written in "litteris Normanno-Saxonicis." In his transcript of the first 30 lines he uses þ, ð, ƿ, ſ, δ, ʒ, and ʒ. The James transcript of the Allen copy also preserves þ, ð, ƿ, ʒ, as well as O.E. ꞃ (*r*), which does not appear in Maidstone, Trinity, or Jesus. Both Trinity and Maidstone give lists of Old English symbols, but in each case the scribes make mistakes in their use, as in the confusion of ʒ with ƿ, or þ with ƿ. The fact that only þ is found in the Jesus version, suggests that the MS. from which the *J.* scribe was copying was not so old as those used by the scribes of the other texts.

SUMMARY OF VALUES

After a consideration of the evidence, we are justified in concluding that Wanley's direct copy of the first 30 lines of the lost Cotton Galba is our most authoritative version. The James transcript of the Allen copy of Cotton Galba, when tested by Wanley's lines, seems to represent a high degree of accuracy. If the lines not given in Wanley are supported by Spelman, we may feel a large measure of confidence in them.

The Maidstone MS., which in its close agreement with the transcripts suggests that it may have been a copy of Cotton Galba itself, or some manuscript not far removed from it, is of the highest

[36] *Op. cit.*, p. 259.

value for the 266 lines it contains.   With the exception of the two transposed sections, it follows the Cotton order; it inserts no unsupported material; and it offers readings which frequently solve unintelligible passages in *T.* or *J.*   Moreover, some of its readings show that it belongs to the parent stem previous to the forking of the Trinity and Jesus MSS.   Its age is also attested by the presence of archaisms, which were misunderstood by the scribes of *T.* and *J.*

The Trinity MS. is next in value, as it is also next in point of time.   Its agreement with the Cotton order, its lack of editorial tinkering, and its large number of supported readings make it very useful.   On the whole, its wording agrees closely with Maidstone. The mistakes which it contains are almost entirely due to scribal error or scribal peculiarity.   It is possible that the copy used by *T.* contained some of these inaccuracies, for the other pieces in the manuscript show fewer mistakes.   Although the *T.* scribe's spellings are sometimes unusual, he had more system than is generally ascribed to him, as for example the use of *st* for *ȝt* and *ht.*   In any case, it is easier to conjecture the original in spite of scribal slips, than to ascertain it in a manuscript where editorial paraphrase, rearrangement, and expansion have taken place, as in the Jesus version.

The Jesus MS., Skeat notwithstanding, seems to be the least valuable of all the texts.   Not only is it a later copy, but it is an offshoot from the direct line descended from the archetype of the *Proverbs.*   This fact is apparent from its extreme divergence from the order prescribed by the other manuscripts, and the other editorial perversions already noted.   It is an interesting MS. since it illustrates the "editorial itch," but should be considered unreliable except where supported by other readings.

On the whole, it appears that the Cotton transcripts and the Maidstone MS. must be depended upon more and more for hints in regard to the archetype of the poem.   In discussing his discovery, Professor Brown says: "It would be idle to speculate as to whether Maidstone was actually copied from the lost Cotton Galba MS., which, for convenience, I have referred to as the archetypal MS. The probability is that several early manuscripts of the *Proverbs* were in circulation of which no record survives.   Nor do I propose now to discuss the question of the date at which the *Proverbs* were composed.   It will be sufficient here to observe that the more archaic forms in the Maidstone text, and the possibility suggested by comparing it with the Trinity and Jesus texts, that other early MSS. were in existence, must inevitably tend to push back the composition of *The Proverbs of Alfred* to a date somewhat earlier than that warranted by previous evidence."[37]

That the date of this interesting Middle English poem is still an open question may be seen from the following summary, which shows, for example, a difference of about 70 years in the dates suggested by Borgström and Hall:

Saxon original	*12th century*	*Early 13th century*	*Mid 13th century*
Kemble[38]	Wanley[39]	Morsbach[44]	Borgström[46]
	ten Brink[40]	Skeat[45]	Wyld[47]
	Wülcker[41]		
	J. Hall[42]		
	J. E. Wells[43]		

[37] *Op. cit.*, p. 259.

[38] Kemble, *The Dialogue of Salomon and Saturnus* (*Ælfric Soc. Pub.*), p. 248. "It is probable that this is derived from a Saxon original."

[39] Wanley's Catalogue in Hickes's *Thesaurus*, p. 231: "circa temp. Henrici II. aut Ricardi I. conscriptum."

[40] ten Brink, *Gesch. der Eng. Litt.*, I, 189.

[41] Wülcker, *Gesch. der Eng. Litt.*, p. 79.

[42] J. Hall, *op. cit.*, Part II, 295: "The composition of the original should, I think, be placed somewhere about 1180."

[43] Wells, *Manual*, p. 375: "The original of these MSS. is probably of about 1150."

[44] Morsbach, *Mittelenglische Grammatik*, p. 10, is of the opinion that the poems of Jesus 29 are "aus dem anfang oder der 1 hälfte des 13 jahrh."

[45] Skeat, *op. cit.*, p. xxxix: "between A.D. 1205 and 1210."

[46] Borgström, *op. cit.*, p. xxiv: "about the middle of the 13th century, i.e., not much earlier than the Trinity MS."

[47] Wyld, *History of Modern Colloquial English*, p. 61.   On p. 61 the conjectured date is 1250, but on p. 37 it is given as 1200—probably a misprint.

CHAPTER II

THE IDENTIFICATION OF SIFORD

THE place-name Siford, which occurs in line 1 of the *Proverbs*, presents the first problem of the poem. It designates the place where the meeting was held at which King Alfred dispensed wisdom. The name shows some variation in the different manuscripts:

> *Sifforde:* Cotton Galba, Wanley's transcript,
> *sifforde:* " " James's transcript,
> *Sifford:* " " Spelman's transcript,
> *siforde:* Trinity,
> *Seuorde:* Jesus.

Unfortunately the Maidstone MS. does not include the first three sections. On account of the agreement of the other manuscripts against *J.*, which is not close to the original, as I have already pointed out, it seems justifiable to suppose that the place-name as given in the archetype was Siford (Sifford).[1] Now if this should prove to be the early form of the name of an actual village, it would support the argument for an earlier dating of the poem; and conversely, if Siford cannot be found in early records, it will greatly weaken the case for an early date. It is my purpose to prove that Siford does occur in records previous to the thirteenth century, and to offer evidence to establish its identity with Shefford of Berkshire rather than with Seaford of Sussex or Shifford of Oxfordshire, as suggested by different scholars.

Spelman, in explaining his transcript of the *Proverbs* contained in the *Life of Alfred*, identifies Siford as *Shifford*, Oxfordshire.[2] Wright makes no effort to locate Siford, but the next editor, Kemble,

---

[1] The doubling of a medial consonant was very common and apparently a matter of taste rather than of rule. At times it was used to indicate a short preceding vowel, as in *Ormulum*. The final *e* in the MSS. is due to the dative form.

[2] Spelman, *Life of Alfred the Great*, pp. 126, 158.

refers to the *Proverbs* as "a collection of wise sayings which that prince [Alfred] delivered to his Witena gemot at *Seaford*, [Sussex]."[3] Morris, in his *Old English Miscellany*, shows by the gloss to his text that he interprets Siford as Seaford.

This theory has now become the popular one. Skeat, in his edition of the *Proverbs* (p. 53), not only identifies the place as Seaford, but adds: "The casual guess that the reference is to Shefford (Berks. or Beds.) is valueless, as the Sheffords are remote from the use of the southern dialect."

The Seaford, Sussex, theory has also been accepted by Joseph Hall[4] and by William H. Stevenson, editor of *Asser's Life of King Alfred*, 1904.[5]

Borgström (p. 46) offers a compromise theory: "The two different readings in the MSS. seem to denote different places. *Seuorde* (Jesus MS.) is the present Seaford on the coast of Sussex. *Sifforde* (Cotton), according to Spelman, is 'sive ea Siffordia . . . in Agro Oxoniensi, (ab Oxonio septem milia passuum), sive alius quilibet locus.' It seems very probable from the spelling siforde (Sifforde), *i* for *e*, that the scribes of the Trinity and Cotton MSS. knew of the place in the neighborhood of Oxford mentioned by Spelman."

SEAFORD, SUSSEX

Since the identification of Siford with Seaford, Sussex, meets with the approval of so many scholars, I shall turn first to a consideration of the evidence in its favor. Its claim rests on the general likeness in name, the appropriateness of a southern location in a poem in Southern dialect, and its proximity to West Dean, a place identified as the Dene mentioned in Asser's *Life* and Alfred's will. The last is the strongest point, although it is not necessarily conclusive. Surely an appropriate setting would be chosen by the compiler of proverbs ascribed to Alfred by tradition or on account of his wisdom. Such a place must be one in a vicinity known to have been connected with Alfred, so that no claim to identity with Siford need be considered among towns too far north to have been frequented by him. On the other hand, the fact that his presence

[3] Kemble, *The Dialogue of Salomon and Saturnus* (Ælfric Soc. Pub.), p. 225.
[4] Hall, *op. cit.*, II, 295.
[5] P. lxxii, note 5.

has been recorded in a certain vicinity will of itself alone not be sufficient proof, since, in his campaigns in Southern and Midland England, he may have been in the neighborhood of more than one town conjectured as Siford.

In his *Life of Alfred*, Bishop Asser tells of his first meeting with the King:[6]

His temporibus ego quoque a rege advocatus de occiduis et ultimis Britanniæ finibus ad Saxoniam adveni, cumque per multa terrarum spatia illum adire proposueram, usque ad regionem Dexteralium Saxonum, quæ Saxonice Suth-Seaxum appellatur, ductoribus eiusdem gentis comitantibus, perveni. Ibique illum in villa regia, quæ dicitur Dene, primitus vidi.

Stevenson says (p. 312) in regard to this place-name: "This villa regia in Sussex is, no doubt, the Dene of Alfred's will, in which it is bequeathed to Edward, the king's eldest son. This seems to be Dean (Eastdean and Westdean), near Eastbourne, which in the time of Edward the Confessor was held by Goda, the king's sister."[7]

Although there is another Dean in Sussex, near Chichester, which was suggested by Conybeare[8] as the royal vill, the fact that the village near Eastbourne was still in the royal family at the time of the *Domesday* survey makes the latter identification more probable. As this Dean is within a few miles of Seaford, we must concede to its advocates that it fulfills the requirement of being in a neighborhood associated with Alfred. It is also located in the area in which the dialect of the poem was spoken. Let us now look at the early records and see if the name occurs as Siford. If the name is not found in that form, the evidence for Seaford will be seriously undermined, and if another town in an Alfredian locality appears in ancient records as Siford, the claim for Seaford, Sussex, will have to be relinquished.

The earliest reference to Seaford, Sussex, does not relate to a town, but to the River Ouse.[9] In a grant made by Duke Berthuald

---

[6] Stevenson, W. H., *Asser's Life of King Alfred*, pp. 63–64.
[7] Birch, *Cartularium Saxonicum*, II, 178, line 7.
Domesday Book, I, fol. 19, col. 1, and fol. 19b, col. 1.

[8] Conybeare, *Alfred in the Chroniclers*, p. 106, note 1.
[9] Mawer and Stenton, *Publications of the English Place-name Society*, Vol. VII, *Sussex*, Part II, p. 363.

in 788 to the Abbey of St. Denis in France, he includes "omnem illam villam meam quæ vocatur Ridrefelda sitam super fluvium qui dicitur Saforda in pago qui nuncupatur Successa."[10] In the confirmation of this grant in 790, Ridrefelda (Rotherfield) is again described as "super fluvium Saforda."[11]

Seaford is not mentioned in *Domesday Book*, although two of the other towns appear. The earliest definite record[12] of the town Seaford which I have been able to find is nearly a century later. It is a grant of land in 1172 to the Chaplain of Lepers dwelling *juxta Safordiam*.[13] The name appears again in the *Pipe Roll* of 3 Richard I, (1191).[14] Here the spelling is *Safford*, as is also the case (with single *f*) in an ancient deed conjectured to be of 7–10 John.[15] An entry for 1203 in the *Liberate Rolls* gives Saeford.[16] In the *Red Book of the Exchequer*,[17] among the Sussex escheats for 1210–12, the name occurs as *Seford*. This form, with an occasional *Safford* or *Seoford*, seems to have been the common designation of the town until the late 15th and 16th centuries. Although the following list is not exhaustive, it will show the usual spelling for the period.

1229 Sefford, *Close Rolls*, 13 Henry III, p. 245.
1230   "   "   "   14   "   " pp. 369–70.
1230 Seford, *Feet of Fines for Sussex*, II, 63.
1231 Safford and Seford, *Close Rolls*, 15 Henry III, pp. 466, 582.
1233 Seford, *Close Rolls*, 17 Henry III, p. 316.
1234   "   "   "   18   "   " pp. 563, 571, 556.
1235   "   and Sheford, *Close Rolls*, 20 Henry III, pp. 215, 219.
1242 Seford, *Close Rolls*, 26 Henry III, p. 432.
1251 Safford, "   "   35   "   " p. 561.
1296 Seford, *Sussex Subsidies, Sussex Record Society*, X, 35.

[10] Birch, *op. cit.*, I, 351, ✳252.
[11] *Ibid.*, I, 361, ✳259.
[12] In a paper, "The Translation of St. Lewinna from Seaford," by W. H. Blaauw, read before the Sussex Archæological Society, May 5, 1847, mention is made of a history written before 1068 by Drogo, a monk of Flanders (*Sussex Arch. Coll.*, I, 47–8). The monk describes sailing along the coast of England and finding shelter at *Sevordt*, which means "ford of the sea." Mr. Blaauw gives no title or direct reference for this history.
[13] *Sussex Arch. Coll.*, XII, 115.
[14] P. 58.
[15] *Catalogue of Ancient Deeds*, III, 43, ✳A4221.
[16] *Rotuli de Liberate*, edited by Thomas Hardy, p. 67.
[17] *Rolls Series*, II, 555.

1297   Sheford, *Close Rolls*, 25 Edward I, p. 82.
13th century   Seoford, *Catalogue of Ancient Deeds*, I, 459.
1316   Seford, *Catalogue of Ancient Deeds*, III, 240.
1404   "   Bishop Rede's Reg., *Sussex Record Soc. Pub.*, VIII, 60.
1458   Seford, *Sussex Record Soc. Pub.*, XXIX, 25.
1492   Seaford   "   "   "   "   "   81.
1521   Seford   "   "   "   "   "   26.
1524   Seeforde   "   "   "   "   "   81.
1543   Seforde   "   "   "   "   "   26.
1589   Seaford   "   "   "   "   "   82.

Since Seaford, Sussex, does not appear in the form found in the *Proverbs*, we shall have to set aside its claims in favor of a town which does preserve this form, if this town can also be shown to be in a neighborhood associated with Alfred.

SHIFFORD, OXFORDSHIRE

The suggestion of Shifford, Oxfordshire, as made by Spelman, need not detain us long.   Its northern location makes it less probable, although not impossible if other evidence were convincing. Hall says (II, 295) in regard to this point: "That it is 'remote from the use of the Southern dialect' does not prevent it from being the place where Alfred discoursed.   But Seaford, a seaport in Sussex, is more likely to have been associated in the popular mind and tradition with Alfred."

I have not been able to find any historical or legendary connections of Alfred with this vicinity.   The first reference to the Oxford Shifford occurs in a charter of King Æthelred given in 1005 to Æthelmar, the Ealdorman, to found a monastery, and to endow it with the manors of Eynsham, Shifford, etc.: "uillam quoque quae Scipford dicitur."[18]

Shifford also occurs in *Domesday Book*, but not as *Siford*.   It appears as *Scipford* in two places.[19]   I find the spelling *Scipfort* in the confirmation of the charter of Eynsham Abbey in 1091 by William II.[20]   In a charter of Henry I of 1109 to the same, the manor is spelled *Scipford*.[21]   There is no mention in the early *Pipe*

[18] Kemble, *Codex Diplomaticus Aevi Saxonici*, III, 341, ≠714.
[19] Fol. 155a, col. 2 and fol. 157b, col. 2.

[20] Dugdale, *Monasticon*, III, 15, 30.
[21] *Ibid.*, III, p. 15, col. 2.

Rolls of the Oxfordshire Shifford, but *Close Rolls* and other records give the following forms:

1231   Sibbeford, *Close Rolls*, 15 Henry III, p. 521.
1234   "   "   " 18   "   "   p. 568.
1235   Sibeford,   "   " 19   "   "   p. 173.
1251   "   "   " 35   "   "   p. 433.
1269   Sypforde, *Extent of Monastery of Eynsham.*[22]
Reign of Henry III, Sibeforde, *Red Book of the Exchequer*, II, 799, Appendix.

Shifford, Oxfordshire, then, does not present even so strong a claim to be the Siford of the *Proverbs* as Seaford did, for the Oxfordshire town not only does not appear in the proper form, but it has no particular Alfredian associations.

SHEFFORD, BEDFORDSHIRE

The possibilities of Shefford in Bedfordshire are also very limited. Although it has been considered, in spite of its more northern situation, no scholar has championed it seriously. In the first place, it is not in a neighborhood associated with Alfred; and in the second, its name is not found in *Domesday Book*, nor, according to Dr. Stenton, in other records until well into the thirteenth century. In his account of Shefford in the Bedfordshire section of his work on place-names, Dr. Stenton gives no record before 1220. At this time the spelling was *Sepford*.[23] Other records are as follows:

1227   Sheford, *Assize Rolls*.[24]
1229   Shipford, *Close Rolls*, 13 Henry III, p. 152.
1247   Shepford, *Feet of Fines*.[25]
  "   Sefford, Unpublished *Assize Roll*.
1248   Shipford, *Close Rolls*, 32 Henry III, p. 103.
1262   Shefford, *Feet of Fines*.
1271   "   "   "   "
1276   Cheford, Unpublished *Assize Roll*.
  "   Sheford,   "   "   "

[22] *Cartulary of Eynsham, Oxford Historical Society*, I, 10 (Series, XLIX).
[23] A. Mawer and F. M. Stenton, *Publications of the English Place-name Society*,
Vol. III, 172.
[24] *Ibid.*, p. 96.
[25] For this and following records, see reference in note 23.

1287   Schyford, Chyford, *Placita de quo Warranto.*
1297   Sheford, *Cal. of Inquisitions Post Mortem.*
1307   Schepeford, Unpublished *Assize Roll.*

Thus it appears that the Bedfordshire town at no time assumes the form of the place-name of the *Proverbs;* therefore its case may be dismissed for lack of evidence.

SIFORD, BERKSHIRE

It is singular that in this quest for Alfred's Siford, no scholar has noticed the fact that *Domesday Book* contains the exact form. The village that is listed there as Siford is the present Shefford of Berkshire.   Here at last, then, is a place, the early name of which actually corresponds to our text.   It is mentioned four times, three of the references applying to land in what is now East Shefford, and one to land in West Shefford.[26]   In all cases the land was earlier held in alod of King Edward, the three holdings in East Shefford going back to King Brictric, who held it of King Edward; and West Shefford to Ulveva, who held in alod of the same.   Two of the feoffs were still held of the king: one in East Shefford by Aiulf, the sheriff; the other in West Shefford by Hugh de Port, a prominent man of the times, who held seventy estates at the time of the Conquest,[27] and whose son, Henry, was a baron of the Exchequer, according to Tanner.[28]

By the time this place-name again appears in legal documents, a change in its form seems to be taking place.   John de Port, the grandson of Hugh, confirmed a grant of his father to the Priory of West Shirburne in which "5 hides of land in Sipford"[29] are specified. This confirmation is undated, but can be roughly estimated by generations.   An entry in the *Red Book of the Exchequer*[30] shows that John de Port was still alive in 1166.   The place-name again occurs in the *Pipe Rolls* of 13–16 Henry II.[31]   These entries refer to the large estate in the present East Shefford, held at that time by Hugh de Doura.   In each of the four years the estate is mentioned once,

---

[26] *Domesday Book*, I, fol. 62a, col. 2; 62b, cols. 1 & 2; 63a, col. 1.
[27] Dugdale, *The Baronage of England*, I, 463.
[28] Dugdale, *Monasticon*, VII, 1013.
[29] *Ibid.*, VII, 1014.
[30] I, 206.
[31] Pages 8, 201, 79, 71, respectively.

and in all cases it is spelled Schipford.   In the *Victoria County History* the name change is indicated as follows:[32]

11th century	Siford
12th "	Siford, Scifford, Schipford
13th "	Schipford, Sipford, Sibeford, Sibesford, Shiford

This shows the general tendency and does not mean that a different spelling never occurs.   *Siford* is the early form; but since place-names change slowly, it would be surprising if it were never found after the 12th century.   That it is so seldom found is good proof that it belongs to an earlier period.

Dr. S. A. Peyton, who is associated with Professor Stenton at the University of Reading, England, kindly sent me a list of the forms in which the name of Shefford, Berks, appears in documents.   I shall quote only up to 1250, as I am not concerned with later changes, when, through the centuries, the *c* and the *p* were gradually eliminated until *Shifford* and finally *Shefford* prevailed.

1086   Siford, *Domesday Book*.
1166–70   Schipford, *Pipe Rolls*.
12th century to 1332   Sifort, Scifford, *I.L.*, II.
1204   Sifford, Hunter, *Fines*.
1206–7   Shiford, Hunter, *Fines*.
1219   Sibesford, *Fees*.
1220   Sipford,   "
"   Estsipford, *Fees*.
"   Westsipford, "
1233   Shipford, *Close Rolls*.
1241   Sifford, *Assize Rolls*.
"   Shifford, "   "
"   West Shifford, *Assize Rolls*.
1242–3   Estsifford, *Fees*.
"   Estseifford,   "
"   Westsipford,   "

This list shows only two *Sifford* forms in the 13th century, except the compound, Estsifford of 1242–3.   As the distinction between

[32] *The Victoria History of the County of Berkshire*, IV, 234.

East and West does not appear until 1220, this addition sets it apart from the simple *Sifford* form. The *Sifford* of 1204 on the *Fines* and the one of 1241 on the *Assize Roll* evidently represent a hang-over from the previous century. That there are only two exceptions, with a possible third in the Sifort of the *I.L.*, supports the statement made in the *Victoria County History* that Siford is an 11th and 12th-century form. The scarcity of records in these earlier centuries makes it impossible to present numerous occurrences of the name, but fortunately it appears in the most important source, *Domesday Book*.[33]

Comparison of the claims of Shefford with those of Seaford, Sussex, its only important rival, shows that the Berkshire town alone can claim the name as it appears in the *Proverbs*. Let us see if it is as appropriate as Seaford in other respects.

Shefford, Berks, is in the second row of counties from the southern coast, and so a little farther north than the area in which the Southern dialect was predominant. This, however, is no vital objection, since a southern writer would not necessarily choose a town in his own district if he knew of an Alfredian tradition connected with another town. To those who still feel that the locality of Shefford, Berks, weakens its claims, I would point out the fact that the lost Cotton Galba manuscript, the oldest of which we have any knowledge, contained some Midland forms, as proved by the transcripts. The Maidstone MS. likewise has a strong Midland coloring, as I shall demonstrate in detail in a later chapter. These facts indicate that the original was not so purely Southern as some would believe.

The point which now remains to be proved, and is next in im-

---

[33] Kemble (*Cod. Dip.*, IV, 79, ✻770) records a land grant of Edward in 1044 to Ordgar, his faithful minister, in which *sehford* is mentioned as part of the boundary. "Concedo in illo loco qui dicitur Benyðan Elddin. . . .Ðys is þære anre gyrde landgemæru be niðan elddin. ærest on sehfrod . . . þonne andlang weges eft to sehford."

I have been unable to identify Beneath Elddin or Lower Elddin. Although an Eldon is to be found in Durham, and an Elveden or Elden in Suffolk, no Elddin appears in the neighborhood of the towns with names approximating Siford. *The Victoria History of the County of Berkshire*, however, mentions (IV, 505) an Eldenberwe among 10th-century place-names found in Ashbury parish, Berkshire, (Siford vicinity). Since the grant in one place refers to *eldin byrig*, there may perhaps be some connection.

portance to identity of name, has to do with the associations of the place. Is Shefford, Berks, in a neighborhood connected with Alfredian history, or is Seaford of Sussex the only claimant that can boast of visitations of the great Anglo-Saxon king in its vicinity?

An examination of the *Anglo-Saxon Charters*, the *Chronicle of Abingdon*, and other documents, shows that the country within a radius of fifteen miles of Shefford, Berks, has not one, but many connections with Alfred. There is no record which mentions the name of the town itself, but neither is there record of any other Siford, Shefford, or Seaford directly connected with the king.

According to Asser, the contemporary biographer of Alfred, the king was born in the royal vill at Wantage within ten miles of Shefford. He says:[34]

Anno Dominicæ Incarnationis DCCCXLIX natus est Ælfred, Angul-Saxonum rex, in villa regia, quæ dicitur Uuanating, in illa paga, quæ nominatur Berrocscire: quæ paga taliter vocatur a Berroc silva, ubi buxus abundantissime nascitur.

Miss Beatrice A. Lees, who has written the most recent biography of Alfred the Great, comments on the passage as follows:[35]

"Isolated as is this mention of Alfred's birthplace, there is no reason to doubt its truth. Its very unexpectedness, indeed, makes for its credibility. Wantage, though a royal 'vill,' was too small and inconspicuous to have been deliberately chosen by an unscrupulous biographer for the scene of his hero's entrance into the world. On the other hand, it was quite a possible place for the birth of a son of the house of Egbert, which held large estates in the neighborhood, originating, possibly, in the grant of land 'about Ashdown' made in the middle of the 7th century by Cenwalh, King of the West-Saxons, to his kinsman Cuthred, grandson of Cynegils, a former king. The ham at 'Waneting' was bequeathed by Alfred to his wife, and remained crown-land till the 12th century. Asser may even have derived his information from the king himself. The local touches, the etymology of 'Berkshire,' the box-trees in the Berroc wood, suggest a special personal knowledge, for it was unusual in the 9th century to preserve details of birth, save in those

[34] Stevenson, W. H., *op. cit.*, p. 1.   [35] Lees, *Alfred the Great*, pp. 61–62.

ecclesiastical biographies where signs and portents heralded the advent of a future saint or martyr."

It is interesting to note that a statue of the great Anglo-Saxon king has been erected at Wantage to mark his birthplace.

Not only was Alfred born at the royal vill at Wantage, but, since his family owned a large amount of land in Berkshire, as a boy, he must have moved over the county from one estate to another. His name begins to appear among the witnesses on the king's charters very early. One such charter is that of Æthelwulf, Alfred's father, to Aldred, his thegn, of land at Æscesbyrg,[36] (Ashbury, Berks, about 8 miles from Shefford).[37] *Ego Æðereð, filius regis*, and *Ego Ælfræd, filius regis* both are found among the witnesses. This charter, of course, may not have been drawn up at Ashbury, but it is one of the many links binding Alfred to that part of Berkshire. In 862, when Æthelred had become king, he granted to prince Æthelwulf land at Wittanham (about 15 miles from East Shefford). This grant is signed by the king himself and also by "Ælfred, frater regis."[38] Æthelsuith, Queen of the Mercians and Alfred's sister, owned land at Laking or West Locking in Wantage, which she granted in 868 to Cuthwulf, the thegn. For this charter, Æthelred, the king, signed as witness, and also *Ælfreð, filius Regis*, (another MS. has the correct *frater Regis*).[39]

During Alfred's reign other holdings in Berkshire are recorded. Since it seems unlikely that a king would be unfamiliar with his own estates, we are justified in assuming that Alfred was at least occasionally in the places for which we have land grants. In one charter, he exchanged for estates in other counties holdings in Cholsey (15 miles from Shefford), Hagborne (11 miles from Shefford), and Besilsleigh (17½ miles)—all in Berkshire.[40] In the latter years of his life he granted to Deormod, the thegn, land at Appelford, Berks (14 m. from Shefford) in exchange for property in another county.[41]

Although there is no charter, the *Chronicle of Abingdon* states

[36] Birch, *op. cit.*, II, 93, ⚹491.
[37] Distances are estimated from map in *The Victoria History of Berkshire*, I, 229.
[38] Birch, *op. cit.*, II, 111, ⚹504.
[39] *Ibid.*, II, 139, ⚹522, also note p. 140.
[40] *Ibid.*, II, 205, ⚹565.
[41] *Ibid.*, II, 223, ⚹581.

that Alfred owned land there (15 m. from Shefford).   Stenton even surmises that the monastery, which was very small, may have been a royal demesne.[42]   At one time the king apparently deprived the monastery of the vill of Abingdon with all its appurtenances.   The chronicler writes wrathfully:[43]

Hic vero mala malis accumulans, quasi Judas inter XII, villam in qua cœnobium situm est, quæ vulgari idiomate Abbendonia appellatur, cum omnibus suis appenditiis a prædicto cœnobio violenter abstraxit, victori Domino, pro victoria qua functus est de Danis super Essedune victis, inparem reddens talionem.

It is possible, however, to come much nearer Shefford in these documents.   In Alfred's will, which is accepted as genuine, the hams at Lambourne, Wantage, and Ethandun are bequeathed to his wife, Ealhswithe.[44]   Lambourne is within five miles of Shefford and was doubtless often visited by the king.   Three holdings are mentioned in *Domesday Book*, one of which was still in royal hands and the other two held by the present owners from the king.[45]

Let us now turn back to Asser to see if he mentions seeing Alfred in this vicinity.   In paragraph 81, of the *Life*, he tells us that he spent eight months with the king at the royal vill of *Leonaford*.

Cum igitur ad eum advenissem in villa regia, quæ dicitur Leonaford, honorabiliter ab eo susceptus sum, et cum eo illa vice octo mensibus in curto mansi, in quibus recitavi illi libros quoscunque ille vellet, et quos ad manum haberemus.

Conybeare identifies Leonaford as Linford, Berks,[46] but Stevenson hazards Landford, Wilts.[47]   Linford, Berks, however, seems much more probable, since it is within two or three miles of the monastery of Abingdon, in the vicinity of which Alfred had other holdings. Moreover King Edmund, the grandson of Alfred, granted 6 hides of land at Linford to a man named Ælfheagus, who

[42] Stenton, *The Early History of the Abbey of Abingdon*, pp. 30–31.
[43] *Chronicon Monasterii de Abingdon, Rolls Series*, I, 50.
[44] Birch, *op. cit.*, II, 176 ff., ✻553.

[45] *Domesday Book*, I, fol. 57b, col. 1; 61b, col. 2; 62a, col. 1.
[46] Conybeare, *op. cit.*, p. 108, note 1.
[47] Stevenson, W. H., *op. cit.*, pp. 318–20.

gave it to the Abbey.[48] This grant and one from King Cnut[49] show that the royal family at one time had holdings here. Linford appears in *Domesday Book*, but by that time it is out of royal hands.[50] If the identification of Leonaford with Linford is correct, it means that King Alfred spent at least eight months within about twelve miles of Shefford.

Not only is the Shefford neighborhood associated with the birth and life of the king, but it is the site of one of the most exciting of his battles with the Danes. *The Anglo-Saxon Chronicle* for 871 reads (in translation):[51]

This year came the army [Danes] to Reading in Wessex; and in the course of three nights after rode two earls up, who were met by Alderman Æthelwulf [of Berks] at Englefield; where he fought with them and obtained the victory. There one of them was slain, whose name was Sidrac. About four nights after this, King Æthered and Alfred, his brother, led their main army to Reading, where they fought with the enemy; and there was much slaughter on either hand, Alderman Æthelwulf being among the slain; but the Danes kept possession of the field.

Different suggestions have been made in regard to the position of the Saxons during the next few days before they returned to the attack. Miss Lees, after mentioning Gaimar's assertion that they went to the East, which she feels is unsupported by other evidence, continues:[52] "It is more likely that the retreat would be to the West, where the royal demesne lands, from the 'ham' at Wantage to the 'ham' at Lambourn across the Downs, would furnish shelter and supplies, or to the South, to cover Winchester, which lies in a direct southerly line from Reading."

The Anglo-Saxon Chronicle continues:[53]

And about four nights after this, King Æthered and Alfred, his brother, fought with all the army on Ashdown [Æscesdune], and the Danes were overcome. They had two heathen kings, Bagsac and Healfden, and many earls; and they were in two divisions; in one of which

---

[48] *Chronicon Monasterii de Abingdon,* I, 106-7.
[49] *Ibid.,* p. 439.
[50] Fol. 59a, col. 1.

[51] Ingram, *The Anglo-Saxon Chronicle,* p. 64.
[52] Lees, *op. cit.,* pp. 118-19.
[53] Ingram, *op. cit.,* pp. 64-5.

were Bagsac and Healfden, the heathen kings, and in the other were the
earls.   King Æthered, therefore, fought with the troops of the kings,
and there was King Bagsac slain; and Alfred, his brother, fought with
the troops of the earls, and there were slain Earl Sidrac, the elder, Earl
Sidrac, the younger, Earl Osbern, Earl Frene, and Earl Harold.   They
put both the troops to flight; there were many thousands of the slain,
and they continued fighting till night.

W. H. Simcox in his article in the *English Historical Review*, 1886,
entitled "Alfred's Year of Battles," interprets Æscesdune as "the
range of open chalk hills called Ashdown which forms an appreciable
part and commands the whole of Berkshire."[54]

Various other localities have been suggested for Æscesdune, such
as Ashdown Forest in Sussex, Ashdown in Essex, and Ashendon in
Buckinghamshire, but these places are inconsistent with the action
which was near Reading, the Danish base.   Miss Lees says (p. 120):
"The claims of Sussex, Essex, and Buckinghamshire are easily
dismissed.   The whole campaign centered in the Berkshire and
Wiltshire hills, and it would require more than the recurrence of a
not unusual place-name to justify its transference to the extreme
south or east of England or to Mercia."

Three Berkshire places have been suggested: Assedone near
Pangbourne, Aston at the eastern end of the Berkshire Downs,
and Ashdown Park in the manor of Ashbury at the western extremity.

Stevenson (p. 238) points out by reference to charters, that Assedone is really Assendene, the last part of the compound coming
from *denu*, valley, rather than from *dun*.   Aston must also be set
aside, since it represents the Old English East-tun.   Ashdown
Park, according to Miss Lees (p. 120), derives its name from its
location on Ashdown Ridge.   She joins Stevenson in believing that
the use of the word Ashdown in the early chroniclers refers to the
range of hills running east and west between the valleys of the Ock
and the Kennet, rather than to any single spot.

This was also the opinion of an early editor of Asser, Dr. Francis
Wise, who wrote in 1738.   He drew attention to the fact that the

[54] P. 221.

Downs were still called Ashdown by the shepherds.[55]   This identification of Ashdown is supported by the Peterborough manuscript of the *Anglo-Saxon Chronicle*, which describes the Danes going *andlang Æscesdune* to Cwicelmeshlæwe,[56] and also by the passage already quoted from the *Abingdon Chronicle*, which speaks of Alfred's victory *super Essedune*.[57]

We need not now concern ourselves with the efforts made to locate the exact site of the battlefield on this ridge,[58] since no sure proof can be adduced, and a few miles east or west make no difference to our argument.   Perhaps Simcox was right in interpreting Asser's "multa millia . . . per totam campestrem Æscesdun latitudinem ubique dispersa, longe lateque occisa corruerunt"[59] as "The whole length of the level ridge of Ashdown was covered with the slain."[60]

The section of Berkshire in which Shefford is located, has proved very rich in its associations with Alfred.[61]   The proximity of Wan-

[55] Wise, "A Letter to Dr. Mead," pp. 20–22.

[56] Earle and Plummer, *Two Saxon Chronicles*, I, 137.

[57] *Op. cit.*, I, 50.

[58] The connection of the White Horse under Uffington Castle with Alfred is very late.   Previous to the time of Dr. Wise, this was associated with Hengist and Horsa, (Stevenson, p. 237).   Stevenson also calls Alfred's Castle, a name given to some ruins near Ashdown Park, an antiquarian figment, (p. 235, note 2).

[59] Asser, paragraph 39, lines 16–19.

[60] Simcox, "Alfred's Year of Battles," *Eng. Hist. Rev.*, 1886, p. 224.

[61] There is some possibility that part of the 878 campaign was connected with Berkshire.   After Easter of that year, Alfred met the men of Somerset, Wiltshire, and Hampshire, at Egbert's Stone. At dawn he marched to a place called * Æcglea* by Asser; *Iglea* in the Anglo-Saxon Chronicle, A, B, and C; and *Æglea* in D and E.   Here the king encamped for the night.   The next day he advanced

to Ethandun and fought.   If the identification made by Professor Beeke of Oxford could be accepted, it would add another Alfredian association to the Siford neighborhood.   Professor Beeke identified Æcglea or Iglea with the place from which the Eglei Hundred of Berkshire derived its name, the site of which is unknown.   He supported this theory by locating Ethandun at Eddington in Hungerford, in this Hundred, (Lysons, *Magna Britannia*, 1806, I, 162).   This is the same Hundred under which Siford is recorded in *Domesday Book*.   W. H. Stevenson, however, objects to Beeke's theory.   He calls attention to the *Pipe Rolls* of 17 Henry II (p. 90) and 18 Henry II (p. 15) where the Berkshire Hundred is spelled Egesleah and Eggesleah, which he thinks shows a derivation from O.E. *Ecges-leah* rather than Iglea. He also proves (pp. 273–275) by various documents that the Berkshire Eddington does not appear as Eðandun, but that Edington in Wiltshire does.   He is, however, hard put to it to find an Iglea in the tage, the birthplace of the king, the existence of the royal vills there and at Lambourne (and perhaps at Linford), and the neighboring ridge of Ashdown where modern scholars are generally united in locating the famous battle of Æscesdune, all show that this district has the closest connection with the life of the great Saxon king.

Since it is historically appropriate, and since the early form of its name as it appears in *Domesday Book*, is identical with the Siford of the *Proverbs*, the claims of Shefford, Berks, outweigh those of Seaford, Sussex, or Shifford of Oxfordshire, and Shefford of Bedfordshire.

Let us now consider how this identification affects the dating of the poem. In the first place, it presents no obstacle to the assumption of a twelfth-century date as would be the case if the *Proverbs* form had been Sibeford or Shifford—spellings not found until the thirteenth century. Conversely, it greatly increases the probability of an early date, since the author or compiler would naturally choose the form current in his own time. As I have already shown, Siford is the eleventh and twelfth-century spelling, which began to change even before 1200.

Moreover, a thirteenth-century writer would have passed over

neighborhood of the Wiltshire Edington. In the seventeenth century an *Iley Oak* is mentioned near Southleigh Wood in that vicinity, and a place called *Ilegh* is spoken of in the fifteenth century. Stevenson (p. 272) surmises that Iglea was "probably an older name of Southleigh Wood or part of it, and that *leah* has in this case its older meaning of *wood*. Southleigh Wood is bounded on one side by the river Deverill, so that the application of *ieg* [island] to it or a portion of it is intelligible."

This identification is perhaps possible, but certainly not convincing. Moreover, although the Edington in Wilts may have been called Ethandun, was it the only Ethandun? In weighing Stevenson's objection to the Berkshire Eglei, it must

not be forgotten that in the Cotton MS. of Asser's *Life of King Alfred*, the spelling was Æcglea, which would be O.E. *Ecg-leah*, from which the forms in the *Pipe Rolls* differ only in the use of the genitive. On the evidence now available, no sure identification of Iglea can be made, although nearly a dozen places have been suggested in different parts of England. The Wiltshire region has the most advocates because of the early *Ethandun* form for Edington and because of its proximity to Somerset, from which Alfred had brought his army. However, evidence may sometime be discovered which will show that the presence of Siford in the Eglei Hundred is more than a mere coincidence.

Siford, an apparently obscure village, and chosen Winchester as a suitable place for this assembly. Alfred used Winchester as his capital, giving judgment,[62] and perhaps issuing his law code there.[63] He founded the New Minster, and with his wife is believed to have established the Abbey of St. Mary in Winchester.[64] This city was also his final resting-place. According to the *Book of Hyde*, he was first buried in Winchester Cathedral, but when the canons were troubled by the walking of his ghost, his son Edward removed the body to the New Minster.[65]

That Winchester was not used as the setting for the poem strongly suggests that the author lived in an earlier period in which tradition associated Alfred with Siford. We know that Siford was settled long before the *Domesday Book* record, because Anglo-Saxon remains have been found near the manor-farm in what is now called East Shefford.[66] During the construction of the Lambourne Valley railroad, 1890, a number of skeletons were disinterred. Weapons, jewelry, and vases from this interment may be seen in the British Museum. Since the Saxons began to bury their dead in church-yards and churches in the eighth century, these remains show that there was a settlement at Siford before that time, and thus prior to Alfred's reign. The antiquity of this village, as well as its location within five miles of Alfred's ham at Lambourne, makes it a very possible place for a folk-moot, some tradition[67] of which appears to have been handed down to the compiler of the *Proverbs*.

[62] *Anglo-Saxon Chronicle*, last part of entry for 897.

[63] Lees, *op. cit.*, p. 327: "The most ancient [MS. of the Code], which was probably copied straight from an Alfredian original, is now bound up with the famous Parker MS. of the Anglo-Saxon Chronicle, and, like it, seems to have come from Winchester."

[64] *Ibid.*, pp. 114, 414.

[65] *Liber Monasterii de Hyda, Rolls Series*, pp. 76, 61–62.

[66] *The Victoria History of Berkshire*, I, 239–240.

[67] In the seventh line of the *Proverbs* there is another possible trace of an early tradition. After the enumeration of bishops, earls, knights, and book-learned men, comes a certain *Erl Alfrich*, the only person except King Alfred who is mentioned by name. Alfrich was too common a name in Alfred's time to admit of certain identification now, but its gratuitous insertion suggests that it had some real connection with early stories of the king. Perhaps this earl was the *Ælfric thesaurarius* who signed as witness to a charter granted by Alfred in 892, (Birch, *Cart. Sax.*, II, 209, ✻ 567).

In view of the author's apparent knowledge of an early tradition, and in consideration of the eleventh and twelfth-century form of the place-name used, I feel that I have obtained some support for a twelfth-century dating of the archetype of *The Proverbs of Alfred*— a period more in accord with the findings in the Maidstone manuscript than is the thirteenth century.

CHAPTER III

EARLY LITERARY REFERENCES

ALFRED'S FAME IN THE CHRONICLES

BEFORE discussing in detail works of literature which may conceivably show the influence of the *Proverbs*, I shall give some account of the way in which Alfred was regarded in the 12th century. The memory of the great Saxon king and leader was cherished reverently, especially by the chroniclers of the earlier part of the century, who, perhaps, were near enough to the Norman Conquest to have a particular appreciation of the state of national unity and enterprise achieved by Alfred in a former age.

William of Malmesbury, the most noted of these writers, devotes a number of paragraphs to Alfred in his *Gesta Regum Anglorum*, 1125. After a description of the victories over the Danes, the chronicler turns to administrative matters and praises the law code established by the king. The division of the people into Hundreds is also ascribed to Alfred. His literary achievements are likewise recorded enthusiastically. William of Malmesbury, after mentioning Grimbald, Asser, and John Erigena, continues:[1]

His collateralibus rex fretus, liberales artes totis medullis indidit, in tantum ut nullus Anglorum fuerit vel in intelligendo acutior vel in interpretando elegantior.

A list of Alfred's translations follows, with an account of the state of learning in England at that time, as described in the Preface of the *Pastoral Care*. Some of the manuscripts of this chronicle contain a particularly splendid tribute to the great king.[2]

Famosus, bellicosus, victoriosus; viduarum, pupillorum, orphanorum, pauperumque provisor studiosus; *poetarum Saxonicorum peritissimus*,

---

[1] William of Malmesbury, *Gesta Regum Anglorum, Rolls Series*, I, 132.   [2] *Ibid.*, 134, note 1. (The italics are mine.)

suæ genti carissimus, affabilis omnibus, liberalissimus; prudentia, forti-
tudine, temperantia, justitia præditus; in infirmitate qua assidue labor-
abat patientissimus, in exequendis judiciis indagator discretissimus, in
servitio Dei vigilantissimus et devotissimus; Angul-Saxonum rex Ælfre-
dus piissimi regis Athulfi filius, viginti et novem annis sexque mensibus
regni sui peractis, mortem obiit, . . . et Wintoniæ in novo monasterio
sepultus, immortalitatis stolam et resurrectionis gloriam cum justis
expectat.

This encomium also occurs in the Chronicle of Florence of Worcester, (d. 1118), and may be original with him.[3] The conception
of Alfred, not only as a leader in war and a law-giver, but as the
champion of widows, orphans, and the poor; the most skillful of
Saxon poets; and the best beloved of his people, always wise and
devout, agrees with that presented in the *Proverbs:*

> ec Alfrede,
> Engle hirde,
> Engle derling. . .
> Alfred, he was on Engelond,
> a King wel swiðe strong;
> he was King and Clerc;
> wel he luuede Godes werc;
> he was wise on his word
> and war on his speche;
> he was þe wisest man
> þat was on Engelond on.[4]
>
> Þus quad alured, . . .
> sone min, ich þe bidde, . . .
> fader be þu wid child,
> ant be þu widewis frend,
> þe arme ginne þu froueren.[5]

Simeon of Durham, whose *Historia Regum Anglorum* ends in 1129,
is most interested in Alfred as the victor of Ashdown, the sagacious

---

[3] Florence of Worcester, *Chronicon ex
Chronicis, Monumenta Historica Britannica*, edited by Henry Petrie, 1848, p. 567.
[4] Wanley transcript, Hickes's *Thesaurus*,
p. 231. (Wanley, however, always uses
þ and *ȝ*, which for convenience I have
here transcribed as *w* and *g*. The
Trinity *þ* has also been written as *w*.)
[5] These lines are found only in Trinity.
They are lines 532, 547, 551–553.

ruler, and the founder of monasteries.[6] Very little is said about his culture. Gaimar, on the other hand, in his *L'Estorie des Engles,* concludes an account of the campaign against the Danes with this tribute:[7]

> Car sages fu e bon guereier,
> Bien sout ses enemis pleisser;
> Nul mieldre clerc de lui nesteit,
> Car en senfance apris laueit;
> Il fist escriuere vn liure Engleis
> Des auentures, e des leis,
> E de batailles de la terre,
> E des reis ki firent la guere:
> E maint liuere fist il escriuere,
> V li bon clerc vont souent lire.
> Deus ait merci de la sue alme,
> E Sainte Marie, la dame.[8]

Henry of Huntingdon, in his *Historia Anglorum,* eulogizes Alfred's character and military ability in verse, a few lines of which I quote:[9]

> Nobilitas innata tibi probitatis honorem,
> Armipotens Alfrede, dedit, probitasque laborem,
> Perpetuumque labor nomen. . .

To these recorders of the "Gesta" of the English kings, Alfred as the conqueror of the Danes and the wise ruler and uniter of his people, is more important than Alfred the writer and patron of letters, and yet the very fact that this phase of the versatile king is not forgotten in the midst of descriptions of battles and campaigns, shows that the writers of the 12th century were much impressed with this side of Alfred's character.

[6] *Rolls Series*, II, 98–120.
[7] " " , pp. 144–45, ll. 3447–58.
[8] Translation from Conybeare, *Alfred in the Chroniclers*, p. 181. "For wise was he and a warrior good; well knew he how to curb his foes. Never was better clerk than he, for from childhood upwards had he learning. A book made he write in English, of deeds, and of laws, and of battles in the land, and of kings who made war. Books a many made he to write, which learned men go oft to read. May God have mercy on his soul, and St. Mary, our Lady."
[9] *Rolls Series*, p. 152.

Reputation as an Author

Before the end of the century, Alfred seems to have acquired some fame as a writer in the vernacular.   Occasional references are found to works purporting to be from his hand; but since the allusions are few and brief, we cannot be sure whether these 12th-century products have any foundation in some lost Anglo-Saxon original of Alfred's, or whether they have merely been "fathered" on him on account of the prestige of his name and his reputation for wisdom.

One such reference is to be found in the *Ysopet* of Marie de France. In the epilogue the following lines occur:[10]

> Pur amur le cunte Willalme,
> le plus vaillant de cest reialme,
> m'entremis de cest livre faire
> e de l'Engleis en Romanz traire.
> Esope apele um cest livre,
> kil translata e fist escrivre,
> de Griu en Latin le turna.
> Li reis Alvrez, ki mult l'ama,
> le translata puis en Engleis,
> e jeo l'ai rimé en Franceis,
> si cum jol truvai, proprement.

Scholars are still searching for this English source of Marie's, and presenting other unroyal Alfreds as claimants for the honor.[11] Whatever may be the facts of the case, Marie's ascription of a group of fables to King Alfred testifies to the reputation which he enjoyed in the 12th century.

It is interesting to note that Mr. H. B. Hinckley believes that Marie's source was also used by the author of *The Owl and the Nightingale*.[12]

Further testimony is offered by Ailred of Rievaulx, a chronicler in York, (1109–1166).   Speaking of Alfred, he says:[13] "Extant parabolæ ejus plurimum habentes ædificationis, sed et venustatis

[10] *Die Fabeln der Marie de France*, edited by Karl Warnke in *Bibliotheca Normannica*, VI (1898), 327–8.

[11] Jacobs, *The Fables of Æsop*, I, 167–8.

[12] Hinckley, "The Date, Author, and Sources of *The Owl and the Nightingale*," *P.M.L.A.*, XLIV (1929), 347–52.

[13] Twysden, *Historiæ Anglicanæ Scriptores X*, ed. 1652, col. 355.

et jocunditatis." The meaning of the word *parabolæ* is difficult to determine. It was used in the Middle Ages in a sense broad enough to include both fables and proverbs.[14] Odo of Cheriton (d. 1247), for example, wrote not only a series entitled *Fabulæ*, but one called *Parabolæ*, some of which were animal fables, although the stories were generally of the exemplum type.[15] On the other hand, the Wife of Bath refers to the Biblical book of *Proverbs* by its old name, *The Parables of Salomon;*[16] and the *Liber Parabolarum* of Alanus de Insulis is a collection of proverbial sayings.[17] The use of the word *jocunditatis* might be considered an indication that Ailred was referring to fables, and perhaps we should see in this allusion some confirmation of Marie's claim for King Alfred.

ASCRIPTION OF PROVERBS TO ALFRED

The theory that Ailred was referring to proverbs in his allusion to *parabolæ*, gains further probability from another source in which proverbs are definitely mentioned. In that part of the Annals of Winchester, ascribed by Luard[18] to the 12th century, a brief description of Alfred's battles, laws, and efforts toward national education, is followed by the statement: "In proverbiis ita enituit, ut nemo post illum amplius."[19] This evidence is especially welcome since it comes from Winchester, a locality with which Alfred was associated both in life and death. It establishes definitely a 12th-century tradition that King Alfred wrote proverbs, and, moreover, wrote them well.

Such a tradition makes it very probable that the archetype of the present *Proverbs of Alfred* was of the 12th century. Ailred has said that Alfred's *Parabolæ* were *extant*. Moreover, from evidence to be found in *The Owl and the Nightingale*, it is safe to conclude that there was a compilation much larger than the one under discussion, or else that there was more than one collection bearing Alfred's

---

[14] Du Cange defines *parabola* as *verbum, sermo*, but does not use the term *proverbium* or *fabula*. The *New Eng. Dict.* gives *comparison, allegory, discourse, speech, talk*.

[15] Hervieux, *Les Fabulistes Latins*, IV.

[16] Chaucer, *Canterbury Tales*, Wife of Bath's Prologue, l. 679.

[17] Migne, *Patrologia Latina*, CCX, cols. 581–594.

[18] *Annales Monastici, Rolls Series*. II. xi–xv.

[19] *Ibid.*, II, 10.

name. In this poem of the 12th, or at least early 13th century,[20] eighteen proverbs are quoted, which are doubtless older than the other material. Eleven of these proverbs are ascribed to Alfred, but only three of the eleven show any correspondence to the text under consideration,[21] although two of the anonymous ones are also somewhat suggestive.

The first Alfredian proverb to show any similarity is found in *The Owl and the Nightingale*, lines 293–97:

> At sume siþe herde I telle
> hu Alvred sede on his spelle,
> "Loke þat þu ne bo þare
> þar chauling boþ and cheste ȝare
> lat sottes chide and vorþ þu go."

This corresponds to lines 410–14 of the Jesus text of the *Proverbs*, and less closely to section 26 in Trinity. J. reads:

> þus queþ Alured:
> "Ne gabbe þu ne schotte,
> ne chid þu wyþ none sotte;
> ne myd manyes cunnes tales
> ne chid þu wiþ nenne dwales."

The Book of Proverbs, IX, 6, and XIII, 20, gives a Biblical base for this, and it is also to be found in substance in the Anglo-Saxon apothegms of Cotton Julius A. II,[22] and in 12th-century and later paraphrases of *The Distichs of Cato*;[23] but the verbal similarity

[20] The date is still disputed, although many scholars agree on the 12th century, and H. B. Hinckley offers evidence to establish 1177–78 as the date: "The Date of *The Owl and the Nightingale*," *Mod. Phil.*, XVII (1919), 247. In his latest article, he is even more definite, dating the composition of the poem between September, 1178, and the following February: "The Date, Author, and Sources of *The Owl and the Nightingale*," *P.M.L.A.*, XLIV (1929), 329 ff.

[21] As noted by Wilhelm Gadow, "Eule und Nachtigall," *Palæstra*, LXV (1909), 20; and by J. W. H. Atkins in the notes to his edition of *The Owl and the Nightingale*, 1922.

[22] Kemble, "Anglo-Saxon Apothegms," *Salomon and Saturnus* (Ælfric Soc. Pub.), p. 258 (＊5), p. 260 (＊23).

＊5 Ne flyt ðu na wið anwilne man, ne wið ofersprecenne . . .

＊23 Ne beo ðu to ceastful; of irsunge wyxt seofung, and of ðære geþwærnesse lufu.

[23] *Early English Homilies from the Twelfth*

between the line in *The Owl and the Nightingale*, "Lat sottes chide and vorþ þu go," and the command from the *Proverbs*, "Ne chid þu wyþ none sotte," suggests a closer interrelation than that of a common source.

The second proverb in *The Owl and the Nightingale* to show likeness occurs at line 1269 ff.:

> Forþi seide Alfred swiþe wel
> And his word was goddspel,
> þat evereuch man þe bet him beo,
> eaver þe bet he hine beseo;[24]
> *ne truste no mon to his weole*
> *to swiþe, þah he habbe veole.*

The corresponding passage in *The Proverbs of Alfred* is found in all three manuscripts: *M.* 138 ff., *T.* 137, *J.* 180. Trinity affords the best comparison:

> þus quad alfred:
> "ʒif þu hauest welþe awold
> i þis werlde,
> ne þinc þu neure for-þi
> al to wlonc wurþen."

The similarity here is very general and perhaps indicates no closer relationship than a proper reaction in both authors to the Biblical parable of the man who built new barns for his treasures and then died on the morrow.

Century MS., Cotton Vesp. D, XIV, edited by Rubie D-N Warner, *E.E.T.S.,* orig. ser., CLII, 3.

Ne flit þu wið anwillne man, ne wið oferspæcne.

Goldberg, "Ein Englischer Cato," (Vernon and Addit. 22283 MSS.). *Anglia,* VII (1884), 165 ff. Cato Major, Bk. I, 10:

> Aʒeynes men ful of wordes
> Stryue þow riht nouht.

The Latin form is: "Contra verbosos noli contendere verbis." These MSS. of the English Cato are of the second half of the 14th century; but the Anglo-Norman paraphrase from which Goldberg believes they are imitated was written in the 12th century by Everard.

[24] Lines 1271–72 appear later in *The Proverbs of Hendyng, Anglia* IV (1881), 180, as:

> þe bet þe be
> þe bet þe byse. (lines 160–61).

The basis is probably the following distich of Cato:

> Cum fueris felix, quæ sunt aduersa caueto:
> Non eodem cursu respondent ultima primis.

J. W. H. Atkins, the most recent editor of *The Owl and the Nightingale*, suggests a third possible parallel: *O. and N.* 761–2 and *T.* 600–1; but although the thought is similar, the expression of it is so different that the passages have no value in proving any inter-dependence.[25]   The likeness of two of the anonymous proverbs in *The Owl and the Nightingale* to parts of *The Proverbs of Alfred* is also general or to be explained by a common Biblical source.[26]

It seems, therefore, that in spite of general correspondences between the two series of proverbs, there is little or no evidence of real dependence.   Even at best there are eight sayings attributed to Alfred in the Debate poem for which no possible parallel can be found in the *Proverbs*.   We may, therefore, assume that the author of *The Owl and the Nightingale* was using a different collection of Alfred's proverbs, somewhat similar in parts, or else that his source contained much additional material now lost to us.

Many of the proverbs ascribed to Alfred in *The Owl and the Nightingale* seem to be reworkings from the popular *Distichs of Cato* and represent Classical rather than Teutonic wisdom.   However, they at least show the reputation of Alfred in the late 12th or early 13th century as a purveyor of moral sentiments.   These *Distichs of Cato* form a possible source for some of the maxims in *The Proverbs*

---

[25] *The Owl and the Nightingale*, 761–2:
　　Vor soþ hit is þat seide Alvred:
　　"Ne mai no strengþe aȝen red."

The Proverbs of Alfred, T. 600–1:
For þe helder mon me mai of-riden
betere þenne of-reden.

[26] Gadow has called attention to the similarity of thought here: *O. and N.*, 769 ff.:
　Uvel strengþe is lutel wurþ
　Ac wisdom ne w[u]rþ never unw[u]rþ;
　þu myht iseo þurh alle þing,
　þat wisdom naveþ non evening.
Lines 787–8.
　Vor þe mon mid his crafte
　Overkumeþ al orþliche shafte.

The Proverbs of Alfred, M. 193 ff., *T.* 192, *J.* 216. *J.* reads:
　Wit and wisdom,

þat alle þing ouer-goþ.
Syker he may sitte
þe hyne haueþ to i-vere.
For þeyh his eyhte him a-go,
his wit ne agoþ hym neuer-mo.
For ne may he for-vare
þe hyne haueþ to vere,
þe [h]wile his owe lyf
ileste mote.
　Atkins suggests a connection between these two forms of the thought expressed in *Galatians*, VI, 7: "For whatsoever a man soweth, that shall he also reap."
O. and N., 1039–40:
　þat man schal erien an sowe
　þar he wenþ after sum god mowe.
Proverbs of Alfred, M., Jms., T. 78–79, *Sp.* 79–80, *J.* 82–83. *J.* reads:
　Hwych so þe mon soweþ
　Al swuch he schal mowe.

of Alfred.[27] It is evident, then, that there would be no incongruity in the hypothesis that the original *Proverbs of Alfred* should be dated as of the 12th century. The reputation of Alfred as a writer in the vernacular, the mention of his proverbs in Winchester records, and finally the ascription of proverbs to him in *The Owl and the Nightingale*, even if these do not correspond to those in our text, make it reasonable to suppose that the archetype of the *Proverbs* belonged to the same period.

TRACES OF THE "PROVERBS" IN EARLY LITERATURE

A poem of any popularity is likely to leave traces of some sort on contemporary literature. Such traces will, however, be difficult to find in early periods where much has been lost or mutilated. Any reminiscence or quotation of *The Proverbs of Alfred* will repay much searching, where the results so frequently prove negative. I have examined the following didactic pieces without detecting any influence of the *Proverbs: Poema Morale, Sawles Warde, Homilies* from Cotton Vespasian A. 22, *On Ureisun of Oure Louerde, On God Ureisun of Ure Lefdi, On Lofsong of Ure Lefdi, On Lofsong of Ure Louerde, Wohunge of Ure Lauerd,*[28] *Homilies* from Bodley 343,[29] from Cotton Vespasian D.,[30] and from Trinity Coll. Camb. B. 14.52,[31] and miscellaneous pieces from Jesus 29,[32] with one exception.

Long Life

The Proverbs of Alfred occurs in Jesus 29, and on fol. 252b of the same manuscript an indication of its influence may be found. The lyric generally known as *Long Life*, which is copied here, opens with two lines closely corresponding to a passage in the *Proverbs:*

> Mon may longe lyues wene
> Ac ofte him lyeþ þe wrench.

[27] Goldberg, *Die Catonischen Distichen während des Mittelalters in der Englischen und Französischen Literatur*, Leipzig, 1883, pp. 10–11.

[28] The preceding poems are edited by Morris, *E.E.T.S.*, orig. ser., vols. XXIX, XXXIV.

[29] Edited by A. O. Belfour, *E.E.T.S.*, orig. ser., CXXXVII.

[30] Edited by Rubie D-N Warner, *E.E.T.S.*, orig. ser., CLII.

[31] Edited by Morris, *E.E.T.S.*, orig. ser., LIII.

[32] Edited by Morris, *E.E.T.S.*, orig. ser., XLIX.

With this compare *Proverbs*, *M*. and *T*. 153 ff., *J*. 160 ff.   *J*. reads:

> Monymon weneþ
> þat he wene ne þarf,
> longes lyues;
> ac him lyeþ þe wrench.

Professor Carleton Brown has informed me that this poem also occurs in the Maidstone MS.   It is found on fol. 93b, following the *Proverbs*, written on fol. 93a.   Musical notes accompany the lyric. Evidently some song-maker has found inspiration in the *Proverbs*, and by elaborating the thought and improving the rhythm, has made a good song out of a few suggestive lines.

The two poems are again associated in Brit. Mus. Addit. 11579, fol. 72b, where the four lines of the *Proverbs* quoted above are given, followed by verses 3–10 of *Long Life*.[33]   This is another indication that the lyric-writer was using the *Proverbs*, and not vice versa.[34] Lines 16–18 of *Long Life* read:

> Ne may no mon þar-to-yeynes
> . . . Mede liste, ne leches drench.

"Ne leches drench" may have been suggested by this passage from *M*. 161–64 or its corresponding form in one of the other texts:

> Nis no wurt woxsen
> in wude ne in felde
> þat efre muȝe þe feiȝe
> fere up-helden.

Unfortunately no date can be assigned to the lyric, *Long Life;* therefore it does not give us a definite *terminus ad quem* for the *Proverbs*.   However, the fact that it makes use of that poem and has become so closely associated with it that the scribe of Maidstone wrote it on the back of the same leaf, shows that some time must have elapsed between the first appearance of the *Proverbs* and the

---

[33] Brown, *Register of Middle English Religious Verse*, II, 195, ⌗ 1310.
[34] The first two lines of this lyric were incorporated into a thirteenth-century Kentish sermon in Laud 471, and at least a hundred years later Dan Michel used the first stanza in the *Ayenbite of Inwyt*.

Maidstone copy. This idea is in accord with the argument for an earlier dating of the archetype.

A possible echo from the "Long Life" passage in the *Proverbs* may be found in the *Ancren Riwle*[35] where warning is given against leaving confession until the last extremity:

> On oðer half, moni mon abit to schriuen him uort þe nede tippe. *Auh ofte him lieð þe wrench*, "Þet he ne mei hwon he wule, þe nolde hwule þet he muhte."

Here the words "Auh ofte him lieð þe wrench," and the emphasis on the uncertainty of life correspond to both the *Proverbs* and the lyric *Long Life*. It is impossible to say whether the author of the *Ancren Riwle* borrowed directly or merely used an expression made current by the popularity of these poems. The *Ancren Riwle* seems to have no other contact with the *Proverbs*. However, the extract quoted above shows an interesting and more direct reminiscence of another Early English piece, the *Poema Morale*, line 35:

> þe wel ne deð þe hwile he mai, ne scal wenne he walde.

The *Poema Morale*, although it shows no influence from the *Proverbs* in its context, was often associated with that poem. On the lower margin of the page containing the text of the *Proverbs* (Maidstone MS.) a couplet from the *Poema Morale* (lines 149–50) has been inscribed, apparently in the same hand. If it were possible to be sure that this was also on the archetype, some argument might be advanced for the priority of the *Proverbs*, since the scribe would have used the selection from the *Poema Morale* as an introductory couplet preceding his text if it had been known to him earlier. However its presence even on a copy shows that the two poems were early placed together in compilations.

The reminiscence of the *Proverbs* in the *Ancren Riwle* quoted above does not give much assistance toward the date of composition of the *Proverbs* since the *Ancren Riwle* is generally assigned to the early part of the 13th century, although Miss Allen[36] argues for a 12th-century date.

---

[35] Morton, edition for the Camden Society, 1853, p. 338.

[36] Allen, "Origin of the *Ancren Riwle*," *P.M.L.A.*, XXXIII (1918), 474 ff.

The Lambeth Homilies

In some of the Old English homilies correspondences to the *Proverbs* may also be found.   The following parallel occurs in the *Lambeth Homilies* (Lambeth MS. 487), assigned by Morris, Morsbach, and Hall to the latter part of the 12th century.[37]   The man who goes to shrift without meaning to repent "biờ al swa is an eppel iheoweờ: he biờ wiờuten feire, and frakel wiờinnen."[38] This same figure is used by the author of the *Proverbs* when discussing the unfortunate consequences of choosing a wife on the basis of outward appearances.   The Jesus MS. (306–7) reads:

> Mony appel is bryht wiþ-vte,
> and bitter wiþ-inne.

This passage occurs in James, Maidstone, and Trinity in a longer form.[39]

In another part of the *Proverbs*, when the problem of choosing a wife is still under discussion, the author says:

> and ofte mon of fayre
> frakele icheoseþ.[40]

A homilist familiar with the *Proverbs* would associate the two passages and might easily combine them for his own purposes.

The idea expressed in this simile is not new, for it is found in the *Parabolæ* of Alanus de Insulis:

> Non teneas aurum totum quod splendet ut aurum,
> Nec pulchrum pomum quodlibet esse bonum.[41]

Kemble[42] quotes several German parallels such as: "Ist der apffel rosenfarb, der wurm ist darinn"; "Schön öpfel seyn auch wohl sauer"; "Rothe Aepfel sind auch faul."   However, the similarity

[37] Morris, *Old English Homilies, E.E.T.S.*, orig. ser., XXIX, xviii; Morsbach, *Mittelenglische Grammatik*, Halle, 1896, pp. 7, 10; Hall, *op. cit.*, II, 312.
[38] *E.E.T.S.*, orig. ser., XXIX, 25.
[39] James 334 ff.: mani appel is uten grene
7 brihte on beme,
7 bitter piờinnen.

Maidstone: *briht, biter.*
Trinity: *moni, wid-uten, brit, leme, ant bittere widinnen.*
[40] *J.* 256–7.   Also *T.* 272–3.
[41] Migne, *Patrologia Latina*, CCX, cols. 585–86.
[42] *Op. cit.*, p. 252.

of form in expressing the idea is much closer between the *Lambeth Homilies* and the *Proverbs* than in the other versions of the saying. No other proverb which I have so far encountered uses the words *wiþuten* and *wiþinnen*, and there is also the *feire and frakel* correspondence mentioned above.   The dependence is difficult to establish, but it seems reasonable to suppose that the earnest preacher on shrift would be more likely to borrow from a collection of proverbs than vice versa.

The following excerpt from the same series,[43] although Biblical in tone, is very suggestive of the *Proverbs*, and may perhaps be an expansion of the ideas on wealth ascribed to Alfred:

. . . . sette us bisne *þas habbe wele to ouer stohwennesse on þisse liue ne beo þu þereuore prud*, ne wilde, ne sterc, ne wemod, ne ouer modi ah þes þe we heoueden mare wele on þisse liue þes we ahte to beon þe edmoddre and þa mare imete al swa hit ure wele nere and *þonkien hit ure drihten þe hit us lende* and don þan monna þerof þat hit nabbet.

With this compare Trinity 138 ff.:[44]

ʒif þu hauest welþe awold
i þis werlde,
ne þinc þu neure for-þi
al to wlonc wurþen.
Acte nis non eldere stren,
Ac it is godis lone.

These two parallel passages, the one on the apple, fair without and *frakel* within, and the other on wealth as the loan of God which should afford no occasion for pride, indicate, I believe, that the 12th-century homilist was pointing his morals with proverbs from the collection under discussion.   This conclusion, in turn, establishes a 12th-century date for the *Proverbs*, if the dating of Morris, Morsbach, and Hall for the *Lambeth Homilies* may be accepted.

Inspection of other Early English homilies has not been fruitful. No real parallels to the *Proverbs* are found in the series in Trinity Coll. Camb. B. 14. 52, although an occasional phrase is suggestive. The 12th-century *Homilies* in MS. Vespasian D. XIV and Bodley

[43] *Old English Homilies*, p. 5.   [44] Also *M*. 138 and *J*. 181.

343, both apparently based on Ælfric, are in Anglo-Saxon and evidently antedate the *Proverbs*. The Vespasian collection contains a chapter on St. Neot, in which some account of Alfred is given, but although the author says that "his word wide sprang," no mention is made of proverbs.

Layamon's Brut

The *Brut* of Layamon is one of the few Early Middle English poems concerning whose date scholars are fairly well agreed. The generally accepted date is c. 1205, although several scholars place it much earlier. Hall has disproved Madden's argument that Layamon must have written after 1173.[45] Traces of the influence of the *Proverbs* on this early chronicle are, therefore, particularly important.

The most unmistakable instance of direct borrowing by Layamon from *The Proverbs of Alfred* has already been pointed out by Skeat, although he argues that the author of the *Proverbs* was the borrower. In the *Proverbs* we read:

> 7 hwider so þu wende
> sai þu attenende
> wurþe þat i-wurþe
> wurþe godes wille.[46]

With this may be compared the sentence with which the *Brut* ends:

> iwurðe þet iwurðe
> iwurðe Godes wille.[47]

The text of Wace's *Brut*, according to the MS. in the Bibliothèque Nationale, offers no prototype for these lines, so that Layamon either borrowed them from the *Proverbs* or, as Skeat believes, originated them himself. In his note on the corresponding line in the *Proverbs* (p. 67) Skeat says:

The direction in line 570 [499 of my numbering], viz. 'say thou, *at the end*,' shows that an explicit reference to that work [i.e. the *Brut*] is

[45] *Layamon's Brut:* selections, Oxford, 1924, p. 67.
[46] *M.* 498–501; so also in *T.* These lines
[47] *Brut*, 32240–41.

here intended.   Moreover, Part II ends exactly here, and the poem once ended here also; . . .

In the first place, it will be noted, Skeat's assumption that the text of the *Proverbs* once ended at this point is directly contrary to the evidence of the Trinity MS., as well as of the archetypal MS. as summarized by Spelman.   Even more surprising is the sense in which Skeat appears to understand these lines: Whithersoever thou wend, say thou *at the end of the poem,* etc.   It is clear, on the other hand, that "attenende" here refers to the end of one's life-experience.   But if the passage is not used with reference to the end of the *text,* it is difficult to see how Skeat can see in it an explicit allusion to the conclusion of the *Brut.*

If there is any significance at all in the phrase "attenende," it offers better support to the view that Layamon was the borrower. Writers have always shown a fondness for concluding their works with an apt quotation, and these lines certainly supply a suitable ending for Layamon's historical poem.   In recording the last days of Briton rule in England, a spirit of resignation to God's will was most fitting and so, thinking not of the end of an individual life-but of the life of a race, he may very naturally have called to mind the precept in the *Proverbs:*

> wurþe þat i-wurþe
> wurþe godes wille.

Again it should be remembered that the *Brut* is a narrative poem, and that, considering its great length, it contains very few moralizing lines.   Being engaged in perpetuating the memory of deeds, rather than wisdom, the author was less likely to originate a proverb than he was to borrow an aphorism to emphasize his point from a body of wise sayings already collected.   On the other hand, it seems unlikely that a compiler of proverbs should have recourse for material to a long narrative poem like the *Brut,* which in its general character is so widely different.

That the passage in the *Brut* is the quotation and not the original is confirmed by a consideration of the preceding context of the two poems.   In the *Proverbs* thirty-eight lines on the subject of old age precede the two lines in question, which form an integral part of and conclusion to the whole subject; whereas Layamon, four lines before the conclusion, is lamenting the loss of power by the Briton kings. After offering varied advice to the aged, the writer of *Proverbs* concludes (*T*. 492–501):

> þanne þanke þi louerd
> of alle is loue,
> ant of alle þine owene liue,
> ant of þe daȝis litht,
> ant of alle murþe
> þad he for mon makede;
> ant hweder so þu wendes,
> sei þu aten ende:
> 'wrþe þad iwurþe,
> iwurþe godes wille.'

These lines represent a complete thought. In contrast to this unity, the last ten lines of the *Brut*[48] give the impression that the author, having finished his subject, has capped it with an appropriate moral quotation:

> & Ænglisce kinges
> walden þas londes,
> & Bruttes hit losedenden:
> þis lond and þas leode;
> þat næuere seoðð en mære
> kinges neoren here.
> þa ȝet ne com þæs ilke dæi
> beo heonne uorð alse hit mæi:
> iwurðe þet iwurðe:
> iwurðe Godes wille.
>
> Amen.[49]

---

[48] Edited by Sir Frederic Madden for the Soc. of Antiquaries, London, 1847.

[49] For a reminiscence see *Chronicle* of Robert of Gloucester, edited by W. A. Wright, *Rolls Series*, I, lines 5136–7. After a reference to the Merlin prophecy of the restoration of the Briton kings, the chronicler adds:

". . . . þis me ssal ȝut yse Ac vpe godes wille it is wanne it ssal be." The *Chronicle* in its present form is dated as late thirteenth century by the editor, (pp. x–xi).

That Layamon, then, and not the author of the *Proverbs*, was the borrower, seems evident first, because a narrative poet would be more likely to borrow from a compiler of proverbs rather than vice versa; second, because the lines are not in the *Brut* of Wace; third, because they make an appropriate ending in accord with a natural tendency in writers to conclude with a good quotation; and finally, because they represent a rhetorical conclusion rather than an integral part of the subject under discussion, as in the *Proverbs*.

The case is made still stronger by the presence in the *Brut* of other apparent references to the *Proverbs*. In lines 8015–18 of Layamon we read:

> Ful soh seide þe seg
> þe þeos saȝe talde,
> ȝif þu ileuest ælcne mon,
> selde þu sælt wel don.

The corresponding passage in the *Proverbs* occurs in *M*. 325 ff., *T*. 325, and *J*. 352. *M*. reads:

> Gin þu nefre leuen
> alle mannes speche
> ne alle þe þinges
> þat tu herest singe.

There can be no doubt as to the borrower here, since Layamon acknowledges his indebtedness to a sage, although he does not name him. This failure may be explained by the fact that the words are put in the mouth of Cassibelaunus, who lived long before Alfred, and so could not quote him directly without committing a gross anachronism. The lines in Layamon, moreover, have no foundation in Wace. In the same speech in the *Brut*, eleven lines later, another sentence occurs which is not given in Wace: "Nu wes þis ilke iseid me to *bi-swiken*," (l. 8029). In the Maidstone MS., four lines after the quoted speech, the same word *bi-spiken* appears. (*T*. uses *bitechen*, altered to *bikechen*, and *J*. reads *bikache*.) This similarity also suggests the influence of Maidstone, or some previous copy, on the *Brut*.

That Layamon was once more the borrower seems evident when we consider the use made of the famous lines from the *Proverbs*, (Wanley version):

> ec Alfrede,
> Engle hirde,
> Engle derling.

The lines from the *Brut*, (6314–15), read:

> Com Alfred, þe king,
> Englelondes deorlig.

Wace mentions Alfred in the corresponding passage, but he does not call him England's darling.   This, then, is a new addition.   Apparently the epithet made a strong impression on Layamon, for there are at least nine other kings whom he thus endears:

Vortimer, þe king, Bruttene deorling,	line 14937
Ambrose Aurelius, þe king, Bruttene deorlig,	" 16273
Arthur, þe king, Bruttene deorling,	lines 24759, 25118, 26088
Gonwais, þe king, Orka es [Orkaneies] deorling,	line 23827
Gonwais, þe king, utlaȝen deorling,	" 24387
Escil, þe king, Denemarkes deorling,	" 23834
Gillomar, þe king, Irisce monen deorling,	" 24379
Cador, þe king, Ardures deorling,	" 24475
Angel, þe king, Scotlondes deorling,	" 25183
Karic, þe king, heore deorling,	" 29009.

In no case is there any equivalent for *darling* in the corresponding passage in Wace.   To Layamon this has now become the conventional epithet for a king.   When a phrase has thus hardened into a formula, it is some distance past its origin, and we must look elsewhere for that.   The word *darling* is not uncommon in Early and Middle English, but it is generally used with a religious significance, or else to mean favorite or minion.   In Alfred's translation of Boethius the word appears several times, but is not applied to kings nor used as an appositive.   A closer comparison may be made with line 393 of the translation of Gregory's *Pastoral Care:* "... bi

Dauide ðæm Godes dirlinge." Similarly in the *Ancren Riwle*
occurs "Dauid, Godes owune deorling."[50] However, the idea of a
Biblical king as God's darling is very different from the idea of a
national king as the darling of his people.   I have been unable to
find the latter thought expressed in early literature except in the
Proverbs and in Layamon's *Brut*.   Since "Alfrede, Engle derling,"
occurs but once in the *Proverbs*, and plays a useful part in making
clear the relation of Alfred to his people in contrast to the purely
conventional formula in the *Brut*, we may assume that this represents the original appearance of the phrase and that Layamon is
again indebted to the *Proverbs*.

Gropp, in his dissertation, has pointed out another case of indebtedness.   The following passage occurs in *T.* 117–121.   It is also
found in *M.* 117 ff. and *J.* 140:

> for god may ʒiuen,
> wanne he wele
> goed after yuil,
> wele after wrake
> se wel him þet mot ascapen.

The *Brut* reads (3608–9):

> After vuele cumeþ god,
> wel is him þe hit habbe mot.

These lines are not in Wace and apparently represent a contracted
form of the Biblical sentiment expressed in the *Proverbs*.

A fifth example of the influence of the *Proverbs* on Layamon may
be noted in the advice given to Uther, *Brut* 17828–9.   In the *Proverbs* Alfred advises his son (*T.* 549–53):

> þad þu þi folck be fader
> ant for louerd;
> fader be þu wid child,
> ant be þu widewis frend,
> þe arme ginne þu froueren.

Likewise Aurelius, who at one time had called together at York his
earls, and thanes, bishops and book-learned men,[51] as Alfred did at

---

[50] *Op. cit.*, p. 56.   [51] Found in Wace.

Siford, and offered them good advice, now on his death-bed sends
for Uther, his brother, and tells him:

> Wærcche uolke for fæder
> hænen to frouere.

In the *Proverbs* occurs this reference to Christ:[52]

> He is one folkes
> fadir ant frowere.

In the *Brut* (19936–7) it is said of Arthur:

> He wes þan ȝungen for fader
> þan alden for frouer.

Although these passages may have some Biblical foundation such
as *Ecclesiasticus* IV, 10,[53] yet taken into consideration with the
other definite examples, they incline us to believe that they represent another impress of the *Proverbs* on Layamon.

With the cumulative evidence before us, it seems absurd to
picture the unknown compiler of the *Proverbs* laboriously culling
five passages suitable for his collection from 32241 lines of narrative.
The almost inevitable conclusion is that Layamon emphasized or
rounded out his stories with direct quotations or paraphrases from
the short and probably well-known *Proverbs*.

This view will throw a very different light on the dating of the
poem. Skeat (p. xxxix), in discussing the date of the *Proverbs*,
uses as his *terminus a quo*, 1205, the time usually assigned to the
first version of the *Brut*. If his theory that the *Brut* is the source
of the direct quotation must be reversed and the *Proverbs* accepted
as the original, then 1205 will become a *terminus ad quem* for our
poem. This evidence will put an end to 13th century conjectures.
Judging from the length of the *Brut*, we must suppose that its composition covered a considerable period of time. Since the passages
corresponding to the *Proverbs* are well scattered throughout, we
may infer that the latter was in circulation before the *Brut* was

---

[52] *T.* 53–54. Also *J.* and *Jms.* 53–54, and
Spel. 51–52.

[53] Be as a father unto the fatherless, and
instead of a husband unto their mother.

begun or shortly afterward. A 12th-century date for the *Proverbs* then becomes the logical conclusion.

We have now the following chain of evidence. Alfred is mentioned in 12th-century records as a writer of proverbs (Winchester Annals); these *parabolæ* were extant at this time (Ailred of Rievaulx); the early poem, *The Owl and the Nightingale*, contains sayings ascribed to Alfred, although not the same as those included in the *Proverbs*. It is therefore probable that the archetype of our poem was one among several collections of maxims passing under Alfred's name in the 12th century. Moreover, quotations from the *Proverbs* in *Long Life*, the *Lambeth Homilies*, and Layamon's *Brut*, fully justify the acceptance of a 12th-century date for the *Proverbs*.

CHAPTER IV

THE LANGUAGE OF "THE PROVERBS OF ALFRED"

THE *Proverbs of Alfred* has generally been considered a Southern poem. Skeat (p. xxxvii), Borgström (p. xviii), and Hall (II, 292), agree in recognizing it as such, although Borgström calls attention to certain Midland peculiarities in the Trinity MS. Wyld[1] and Jordan[2] both include the *Proverbs* in their list of Southern monuments, Jordan tentatively assigning it to Sussex. He says: "Für die Lokalisierung spricht Seaford v. 1, vielleicht Spur von *y > e*, doch ist die Mundart nicht treu bodenständig."

The Midland coloring noted by Borgström in the Trinity MS. is even more pronounced in Maidstone, the dialect of which has not been previously discussed. To judge by the transcripts, the lost Cotton MS. was also strongly tinged with Midland. I propose to examine the Maidstone and other texts to ascertain to what extent the Midland element is present, and to offer from my findings some suggestions for the original home of the different manuscripts and the possible localization of the archetype.

In order to have at hand a standard for judgment before presenting examples from the different MSS., I shall summarize the Middle English dialect tests suggested by Henry Cecil Wyld in his *History of Modern Colloquial English.*[3] It will not be necessary to include tests for distinguishing Northern forms from those south of the Humber, since with one or two exceptions, the dialectic features of all the manuscripts are obviously South Midland or Southern. Late thirteenth or fourteenth-century developments have also been omitted, since the dates of the MSS. give us a *terminus ad quem* previous to this.

---

[1] Wyld, *History of Modern Colloquial English*, p. 61.

[2] Jordan, *Handbuch der Mittelenglischen Grammatik*, Heidelberg, 1925, p. 7.

[3] Chapter II.

I. Old English *ǽ* in East Midland becomes *ǎ*, or when length-
ened, *ā*. In the South it remains *ǽ* or becomes *ea* or *e*.

II. a. Old English *ǣ*[1] (primitive vowel) is represented by a tense *e*
(*ē*) in East Midland and Kent, but by a slack *e* (*ę*), or *ea* in
the South.

b. Old English *ǣ*[2], the i-umlaut of *ā*, is represented in Middle
English by a slack *e* in all dialects except Kentish, which
has a tense *e*. This test is, therefore, of no value in distinguishing Midland and Southern texts free from Kentish
influence.

III. Old English *ȳ* becomes *ǐ* in East Midland, except near Kent
where it is *ě*. The Southern dialect represents this sound
by *u*, *ui*, or *uy*, although an area in Devon and the Southwest
shows *ǐ* forms. *Ě* is found in Kent.

IV. Old English *ěo* is written *ě* in East Midland; and *eo*, *u*, *ue*, *o*
in the South and Southwest Midlands; *ie*, *ye*, *io*, *yo*, *e*, or *ee*
in Kent. The Southwest is particularly characterized by
the *u*-form.

V. Old English fracture *ea* before *r* plus a consonant becomes
ar in Midland and *er* in the South, and *ear*, *ær*, or *er* in Kent.
Before *ll*, Old English *ea* becomes *all* in Midland, *æll* or *ell*
in the South, and *eall*, *æll*, or *ell* in Kent, but the Midland
all crept into Southern texts very early.

VI. Old English *ea* before *ld* appears as *old* in Midland, as *eald*,
æld, *eld* in the South and Kent, but Midland forms are
borrowed even in the 12th century.

VII. Old English *ǐe* is represented by *e* in the Midlands and Kent,
and by *i*, *u*, *ui*, *uy* in the South.

VIII. The present indicative plural is *es* in the North, *en* or *e* in
Midland, and *eþ* or *iþ* in the South, and *eþ* in Kent.

IX. The present participle ends in -*and*(*e*) in the North, -*end*(*e*)
in the Midlands, and -*ind*(*e*) in the South. The usual form
in Kent is -*ind*(*e*), with occasional -*end*(*e*). The -*ing* and
-*yng* forms of the Midland and South are not found until
later (c. 14th century).

X. The Midland forms of the present indicative plural of *to be*
are *ben*, *aren*, *are*. In the South *beoþ*, *beþ*, and *buþ* are found.
Kent has *bieþ* in addition to the Southern forms.

XI.　In Early Middle English the -*n* suffix of the past participle of strong verbs was retained in the Midland dialect, but generally dropped in the South and in Kent.

The Old English *ge-* prefix in the past participle was dropped in the North and East Midland, but retained longer in the South, the Southwest Midlands, and Kent, commonly in the form of *i-* or *y-*.

XII.　The -*n* of the infinitive is usually retained in the Midlands; its loss is a typical Southern feature. Infinitives ending in -*y*, or -*i*, or -*ie* are characteristic of the South. Infinitives in -*ie* and -*y* are frequent in Kent.

Test 1

When subjected to Test 1—the change of *ǽ* to *a* (Midland), and *ǽ* to *e* (Southern)—all the manuscripts of the *Proverbs* show the Midland *a* in *acres* (*akeres*, etc.), *after*, *appel*, *at*, *fader*, *hwat*, *war*, and usually *þat*. The following list shows cases in which the MS. readings differ:

OLD ENGLISH	MAIDSTONE	COTTON TRANSCRIPTS	TRINITY	JESUS
Ælfrēd		Alfred *or* Alured	Alfred *or* Alured helfred, 71, 95	Ealured, 9, *elsewhere* Alured
Ælfric		Alfrich, 7	alfred, 7	Alurich, 7
æþeling	aþeling, 72	aþeling, 72	heþeling, 72	eþelyng, 74
cwæþ		cѳað, 25 (*Sp.* qwaþ)	quad	queþ
dæges (*gen. s.*)	daies, 495		daȝis, 495	
fæste		faste, 409	faste, 409	
gædeling	gadelig, 342		gadeling, 342	gedelyng, 312
glæd			glade, 48	gled, 304 glednesse, 48
gærs, græs	gras, 103	ȝras, 103	gres, 103	gres, 126

OLD ENGLISH	MAIDSTONE	COTTON TRANSCRIPTS	TRINITY	JESUS
hæfdest	hauedest, 218, 288		hauedest, 242, 288 heuedest, 218	heuedest, 276
hæfde	hauede, 98, 100	hauede, 100	heʒed, 100 (heþed)	hadde, 123
hwænne (hwonne)	hƿanne	þanne	þanne, *usual* þenne, 171	hwanne, *usual* hwenne, 175
næfð			nauid, 461	
næfdest	nahtest, 242		neþedest, 383	
þænne (þonne)	þanne		þanne, *usual* þenne, 159, 244, 601	þanne, *usual* þenne, 112, 114, 166
þæt	þat, þath	þat	þat, þad	þat, *usual* þet, 232
wæs		þas	þas	wes
wræc-sīð	wrakesih, 120		þrake se, 120	

The evidence offered above proves that in this feature the Maidstone MS. and the Cotton transcripts are consistently Midland, that the Trinity MS. is largely Midland, although showing the Southern forms *helfred, hepeling, gres, heuedest, heʒed, nepedest,* and occasionally *þenne* and *penne* for *þanne* and *panne.* The Jesus version, although agreeing with the other MSS. in certain words (see above), shows its Southern character by the use of many *e*-forms in contrast to the parallel *a*-forms in the Maidstone and Cotton transcripts.

TEST 2

Of the 46, or more, different words in the *Proverbs* which derive from Old English $æ$ stems, 20 are of the $æ^2$ type, i.e., $æ$ as the i-um-laut of $ā$. As this became Middle English slack *e* in both Midland and Southern dialects, it will be of no value in distinguishing the manuscripts of the two areas. The $æ^1$ type, which became tense *e* in the Midlands and slack *e* in the South, is represented in manuscripts by the same orthographical symbol *e*, except an occasional *ea* spelling for the slack *e*.[4] We are, therefore, almost entirely dependent on the rime-words to ascertain the proper sound of the vowel. Moreover, these must be rime-words of a different type in order to offer a set standard for pronunciation. Often the word in question does not occur at the end of the line, or if it does, it may not be rimed, since the poem is, as a whole, alliterative rather than riming. I have noted only 14 rimes in which a word derived from O. E. *æ* is a member, and in only 11 of these is the *æ*[1] type found.

Old English

1. afæred   *T.* 655, *aferd* rimes with *werd* (O. E. werod). Slack *e*.

2. dæd   a. *M.* 75, *Jms.* 75, *Sp.* 75, *J.* 77, *deden*, *T.* 75, *dedin* rimes with *leden*, *æ*[2] type. Slack *e*.

         b. *J.* 322, *dede* appears to rime with *arede* two lines above. Slack *e*.

3. ræd   a. *T.* 640, *red* rimes with *red* (color). Slack *e*.

         b. *J.* 124, *reade*. Slack *e*.
         Corresponding passages in *T.*, *Jms.*, and *M.* give *rede* with no indication of pronunciation.

         c. *T.* 662, *red* rimes with *quet* (qued). Tense *e*.

         d. *Jms.* 440, *red* rimes with *led* (O. E. lēod). Tense *e*.
         T. 440, *red* shows assonance with *lede*. Tense *e*.

         e. *J.* 336, *red* rimes with *iseyd*. Tense *e*.
         J. 338, *rede* rimes with *vnlede*, but the latter is of the same type.

         f. *T.* 434, *reid* rimes with *isait* (isaid). Tense *e*. Also 599, *reides*.
         J. 330, (corresponding passage), *red* rimes with *i-sed*. Slack *e* ?

         g. *T.* 372, *reden* rimes with *neden* (O. E. nēod). Tense *e*.

4. stræt   *T.* 575, *stretes* rimes with *metes*. Tense *e*.

The number of instances in the *Proverbs* is not sufficient to make Test 2 of great value; nevertheless, the Southern character of the Jesus MS. may be noted, in contrast to Trinity, which contains more Midland forms. The fragmentary nature of the Maidstone

---

[4] O.E. *æht* appears in *Jms.* as *ehte*,   *athte*, 267, 270.   Cf. *ahte*, *M.* 142. but in *T.* as *hachte*, 410, *haite*, 624, and

MS. and the Cotton transcripts cuts down the number of examples to such an extent that no judgment can be formed. The results of the test may be summarized as follows:

Midland Tense e

	TOTALS
Maidstone	0
James, *red*, 440	1
Spelman	0
Trinity, forms of *red* or *reden*, 372, 434, 440, 599, 662; *stretes*, 575	6
Jesus, *red*, 336	1

Southern Slack e

Maidstone, *deden*, 75	1
James, " 75	1
Spelman, " 75	1
Trinity, *aferd*, 655, *dedin*, 75, *red*, 640	3
Jesus, *deden*, 77, *dede*, 322, *reade*, 124, *red*, 330	4

TEST 3

The results of Test 3 are given in the following table:

Midland, O.E. ȳ to ĭ, (near Kent, e)

OLD ENGLISH	MAIDSTONE	COTTON TRANS.	TRINITY	JESUS
cyning, cyng	king, 73	cinȝ, kinȝ, 12, 18, 63, etc.	king, 12, etc.	king, 19, *etc.*
			kinc, 36 kinhis, 2	
cynn	kinne, 489			
cyrice				chirche, 91
Dryhten	Drichtin, 169 Drihten, 180	drihten, 42, 405	dristin, 42, 180 Drittin, 169 drichen, 405 driȝten, 558	
dysig, dysian	disiȝeþ, 251 desiȝeþ, 253		desi, 299 desiet, 251 desiende, 253	
forhȳdan	for-hidet, 219			

OLD ENGLISH	MAIDSTONE	COTTON TRANS.	TRINITY	JESUS
forþȳ	for-þi, 140		for-þi, 140, 457	for-þi, 422
fylstan			filsten, 563	
fyrst			first, 238, 593	
gehȳdan, gehȳdd			hid, 410	
gemynde			minde, 560	
gewyrcan	iwerche, 107		þerchin, 134	
wyrcan	wirche, 134		þerchet, 253 yperche, 107	
lȳtel	litel, 227, 255 liten, 151?		litil, 227 littele, 639	litel, 395
lȳðre			leþere, 349	
myltan			melten, 506	
nyllan				nele, 358
ofþyncan		ofþincheþ, 420	of-þinket, 420	
rȳman	rimen, 166		rimen, 166	
wyrsa	þersse, 261		þerse, 262	
yfel	iuel, 274 iuele, 112, 119, 263	ifel, 274	iuel, 274, 354 iuele, 271, 277 iþil, 662	
yrre	erre, 182		erre, 182	

Southern, O.E. ȳ to u, ui, or uy

OLD ENGLISH	MAIDSTONE	COTTON TRANS.	TRINITY	JESUS
befȳlan			bi-fulit, 617	
behȳdd				by-hud, 243
cynn			cunnes, 489 cunne, 505	cunnes, 384
cyrice		churche, *Jms.* 87 chureche, *Sp.* 87		
cysta				custe, 252
cȳþan	cuþen, 331		cuþe, 269?	cuþe, 358 cuþeþ, 253

OLD ENGLISH	MAIDSTONE	COTTON TRANS.	TRINITY	JESUS
dysig	dusi, 299			
fyrst	furst, 238			
gebȳrian				ibureþ, 75
gefyrn				ifurn, 335
gehȳdan, gehȳdd		ihud, *Jms.* 410		
gemyltan				i-multen, 385
gewyrcan wyrcan	þurcheþ, 253	iþurche, 107	þurchen, 396, 430	iwurche, 130, 374
			þurche, 519	wurcheþ, 398
hlȳd?			luden, 646	
			vn-luden, 648	
hlysnan			lusninde, 605, 613	
hlystan		lusten, 28	lustin, 28	lusten, 28
			lust, 188	lvsteþ, 212
lȳtel			lutel, 508	lutel, 387, 431
			lutil, 151, 255	
			lutele, 516	
			luttele, 641	
lȳðre			luþere, 388, 605, 610, 613	luþre, 364
mycel	mucheles, 261		muchil, 261	
			ouer-mukil, 392	
myrgþ	murhþe, 496		murþe, 496	
nyllan				nule, 106, 295
wynn				wunne, 390
wyrm			þurmes, 504	
wyrt	þurt, 161		þurt, 161	wurt, 168
yfel			huuele, 112	vuel, 258, 294, 316
				vuele, 261, 287
				vuelne, 330
yrre				vrre, 205

These statistics again show the Midland character of the Maidstone MS., although the occurrence of seven Southern forms and four forms found in the Midland neighboring on Kent or in Kent itself, would place the manuscript on the Southern border of the Midland district. The Cotton transcripts have the same number of Midland and Southern forms, although so few words derived from Old English *y*-stems are present in these incomplete versions that the results of this test are not very certain. The Trinity MS. is also more Midland than Southern, but seven of the examples of Midland forms contain *e*, thus showing strong Kentish or Southeastern influence. The Jesus MS. has few *i*- or *e*-forms, thus exhibiting its usual Southern character.

TEST 4

Old English *ĕo* becomes *e* in East Midland, and *eo*, *u*, *ue*, or *o* in the South, Southwest, and West Midlands.

East Midland e

OLD ENGLISH	MAIDSTONE	COTTON TRANS.	TRINITY	JESUS
bēon	ben, 261	ben, 64, 360	ben, 355,360, *etc.*	
beorcan		berce, 612	berke, 612	
betwēonum	bi-tꝥenen, 305		bituenen, 305	
ceorl		cherl, 88	cherril, 88	
cēosan		chesen, 266	chesen, 266, 444 chesed, 273 ches, 604, 621, 638	
dēore	dere, 474	dere, *Sp*. 38	dere, 189, 548, 566, 603, 620	
dēorling		derlinȝ, 11	derling, 11	
drēorig			dreri, 279	
eorl	erl, 72	erles, 5 erl(e), 7 erl, 72	herles, 5 erl, 7 herl, 72	
eorþe	erþe, 103	erðe, 103	erþe, 103	
feoh	fe, 149		fe, 149, 380	

OLD ENGLISH	MAIDSTONE	COTTON TRANS.	TRINITY	JESUS
fēond	fend, 308		fend, 308	
feorh	fere, 164			
forlēosan	for-leseþ, 184		forlesed, 184	forleseþ, 208
frēo			fre, 367	fremannes, 417
frēond	frend, 107, 309, 474, 481	frend, 38	frend, 107, 300, 309, 366, 474, 481	
		frende, 107		
gestrēon	stren, 142		stren, 142	
grēowe	grewe, 102	ȝreþe, 102	gre[þe], 102	
hēo (she)		he, 340, 612	he, 278, 289, etc.	he, 262
heonan	henne, 166		henne, 166, 168, 482	
	heþen, 168, 482			
heorte	herte, 219		herte, 219, 222, etc.	
hrēoh			rei, 641, 652	
hrēowan	reþen, 236		reþen, 236	rewe, 111
hund-seo-fontig	hundt, seu-enti, 99	hunt-seu-enti, 99	hunt-seu-inti, 99	hundseu-enti, 122
lēod		led, 439	lede, 439	
		lede, Sp. 40	leden, 27, 571	
			ledin, 39	
lēof			lef, 189	
			leue, 533, 637	
			leþe, 620	
lēogan	liȝen, 156		leȝen, 156, 392	
			liȝen, 629	
lēosan			lesen, 390	
leoðu-bīge			leþe-bei, 651	
nēod			nede, 394	
			neden, 373	
smeortan			smerten, 583	
			smerteþ, 654	
tēona			tene, 363	
ðēof			þef, 663	

OLD ENGLISH	MAIDSTONE	COTTON TRANS.	TRINITY	JESUS
þeotan			þeþ[t]it, 658	
un-meoc (*E.M.E.*)			vn-meke, 467	
weorc		ƿerc, 20 werk, *Sp.* 20	ƿerc, 20 ƿerke, 22	werk, 20 werke, 22
weorold (worold)	werlde, 129, 139	ƿerldes, 31 werlde, *Sp.* 59	ƿerelde, 31 ƿerlde, 129, 139, 544 ƿerldes, 503	

Southern or Southwestern eo, u, ue, or o

OLD ENGLISH	MAIDSTONE	COTTON TRANS.	TRINITY	JESUS
bisceop		biscopes, 3	biscopis, 3	Biscopes, 3
ceorl				cheorl, 92
cēosan				cheose, 249 icheose, 341 icheoseþ, 257
dēorling				durlyng, 11
drēorig				dreori, 263
eorl				eorl, 7, 74 eorles, 5
eorþe				eorþe, 126, 262, 436
fela (feola)				fela, *usual* feole, 4, 353
feoh				vouh, 192
feorh				furþ, 171 ?
fortēon				forteoþ, 334
frēond	frond, 300			freond, 38, 130
geogoð	ȝuȝþe, 135 ȝuþe, 127		ȝueþe, 135 aȝueþe, 127	youhþe, 149 youþe, 157
geong	hwungman, 111		ȝung, 348	yong, 134, 287
			ȝunge, 572	yonge, 452
georne				yeorne, 101, 107

Old English	Maidstone	Cotton Trans.	Trinity	Jesus
gestrēon				ìstreon, 185
getrēowe				treowe, 295
grēowe				greowe, 125
hēo (*she*)			hue, 285, 425, 431, *etc.*	heo,277,279, 283, *etc.*
				heoseolf, 426
				heo, *pl.*, 116
heonan				heonne, 173, 175
heorte				heorte, 243, 246
hrēowan				reowe, 456
lēod				leode, 27, 40, 212, 370
lēof				leof, 370
				leoue, 38
lēogan				(lyeþ, 163)
leornian				leorny, 107
				leorneþ, 101
lēoð ?				l[e]oþ, 333, *rimes with* forteoþ
nēod	nude, 345			neode, 213, 316, 372
smeortan				smeorte, 244
tēona				to-teone, 303
trēowþ			tropþe, 375	
þēod				þeode, 369
un-meoc (*E.M.E.*)	un-muke, 467			
weorold (worold)			þorolde, 59	worldes, 31, 151
				world, 182, 382
				worlde, 59

OLD ENGLISH	MAIDSTONE	COTTON TRANS.	TRINITY	JESUS
weorð, unweorð	un-þurþ, 345 un-wurh, 97	unþurð, 97	þord, 643 vnþurþ, 388	wurþ, 314 vnwurþ, 120, 364
weorþan (wurðan)	þurþen, 141 178, etc.	þurden, 359	þurþen, 141, 178, 232,etc.	ny-wurþe, 184
geweorþan	þurþe, 500, 501		iþurþe, 500, 501	iwurþe, 263, 299, etc.
	i-þurþe, 500		þurþu, 281, 298	wurþ, 269, 304
	þur-þu, 281, 298		i-þurþen, 518	
			þorþe, 592	
weorþian (wurðian)		wurthend, Sp. 60	þrþin, 60	wurþie, 60, 404
			þurþen, 525	
weorðscipe		þurðscipe, 32	þrsipe, 32	wurþshipes, 32

Here again the East Midland character is pronounced in the Maidstone, Cotton, and even the Trinity MSS., whereas the Jesus MS. is strongly Southern or Southwestern. In the South, Southwest, and West Midlands, according to Wyld,[5] Luick,[6] and Wright,[7] the ö sound remained long after the North, East, and South Midlands had unrounded it into e, and was written eo until the influence of Anglo-Norman orthography resulted in the spellings u, ue, or o. With the exception of a few instances in Trinity, all the Proverbs MSS. use u following w and preceding rþ. This form, however, was common in Old English, and although it shows the influence of West Saxon, the dialect which was practically received as the standard for the earlier times, yet by the Middle English period its use was not limited to the West. The Peterborough Chronicle and Ormulum, Midland and North Midland pieces, both afford examples.

[5] Wyld, op. cit., p. 34.
[6] Luick, Historische Grammatik der Englischen Sprache, I, 133.
[7] Wright, An Elementary Middle English Grammar, p. 32.

TEST 5

ea before *r plus a consonant*, or before *ll*

The Maidstone MS. uses the Midland forms *all, areʒe, þarf*, but the Southern *bern*. The Cotton transcripts are represented by two examples only, *alle* and *arme*, which are Midland. Trinity has *all, areʒe, arme, armþe, baren, þarf*, but also Southern *middellert*. The Jesus MS. always uses the Midland *þarf* and *all* (the latter was common in the South very early), but Southern *bern* and *erewe*, although also *arewe*, as indicated in the following table:

	Midland				Southern			
OLD ENG.	MAID.	COTTON	TRIN.	JES.	MAID.	COTTON	TRIN.	JES.
bearn			barin, 548 baren, 584		bern, 226, 231, 239, 243			bern, 430
eall	al, alle	alle	al, alle	al, alle				
earg	areʒe, 204, 212, 220, 221		areʒe, 204, 212, 220, 221	arewe, 228				erewe, 236
earm		arme, 39	arme, 39, 553					
earmþu			armþe, 411					
middangeard							middel-lert, 510	
þearf	þarf, 154, 248, 318		þarf, 154, 248, 318	þarf, 161, 345				

TEST 6

In this test all the manuscripts show Southern characteristics; but they have sporadic Midland forms, with the exception of the Cotton transcripts.

Midland, O.E. *ea* before *ld* to *a* or *o*

OLD ENGLISH	MAIDSTONE	COTTON TRANS.	TRINITY	JESUS
healdan			holden, 70, 409 holdin, 132	holde, 72, 154, 422
wealdan	ƿoldest, 472		aþold, 138	wolde, 389

Southern, O.E. *ea* before *ld* to *e* or *ea*

OLD ENGLISH	MAIDSTONE	COTTON TRANS.	TRINITY	JESUS
eald			helde, 573 (*adj. as sb.*)	
healdan	helden, 132, 311 up-helden, 164 ƿiþ-helden, 296	helden, 70, 409	helden, 311, 324, 579	
wealdan	welden, 150, 233, 466 ƿeldest, 226 welde, 115	ƿelden, 32, 415	ƿelden, 150, 233, 296, *etc.* ƿeldin, 32 ƿeldest, 226, 472, 509 ƿelde, 115	welden, 193 welde,32,138, 284 awelde, 442 weldest, 182

TEST 7

O.E. *ie* to Midland *e* and Southern *i*, *u*, *ui*, or *uy*

Maidstone, the Cotton transcripts, and Trinity, with one exception each, are free from Southern forms. The Jesus MS. shows a number of Midland *e*'s, but contains 5 *u*-forms, which usually indicate the Southwest. However, Mr. Hall (II, 292) points out that *ihure* and *ihurd* are found in the *Poema Morale*, "which is generally taken as of the Middle South."

Midland e

OLD ENGLISH	MAIDSTONE	COTTON TRANS.	TRINITY	JESUS
begietan			bi-ȝete, 366	
cierran	chariweþ, 81	charigeþ, 81	cherried, 81	
forgīeman				for-yemeþ, 207
forgietan				for-yeteþ, 208
gelīefan	leuen, 325 lef, 174		ileuen, 649 leuen, 325 leue, 174	ilef, 196, 352
gesīene				isene, 115
giefan			ȝef, 576	yeue, 140
hīeran, ge- hīeran	iheren, 315 herest, 328	heren, 14, 418	heren, 418 i-herin, 14 herest, 328	iherest, 355
hierde			herde, 10	
ieldu	elde (sb.), 131, 235, 463, 471		helde (sb.), 131, 235, 471, 486 elde (sb.), 463	elde (sb.), 104, 110, 112, 153
ieldra (sb.)	eldere, 142		eldere, 142	
ieldra (comp. adj.)			helder, 600	
ieldan	elden, 465		helden, 465	
ierre (yrre)	erre, 182		erre, 182	
scīene	scene, 339	scene, 339	schene, 339	schene, 310
stīeran	sternen, 491		steren, 491	

Southern i or u

cierran				churreþ, 85
giefan	iȝiuene, 128		ȝiuen, 112	
hīe (acc. f.)				hi, 275
hīeran				i-hure, 14 ihurd, 300
hierde		hirde, 10		hurde, 10

OLD ENGLISH	MAIDSTONE	COTTON TRANS.	TRINITY	JESUS
ieldu				(ealde, *sb.*, 441, 455)
ieldra (*sb.*)				ildre, 185
ierre				vrre, 205

TEST 8

One of the best tests to distinguish Midland and Southern texts is found in the ending of the present indicative plural. In the Midlands it is *en* or *e*; the South uses *eþ*, *iþ*, or *þ*. Of the 8 present plurals which occur in the Maidstone MS.,[8] 4 end in *en*, 4 in *e*, and none in *eþ*; so in this respect Maidstone is entirely Midland. The Cotton transcripts are also Midland in the few present plurals included, and so is the Trinity MS., with one exception. Jesus, on the other hand, exhibits the usual Southern *eþ* in all cases.

MAIDSTONE	COTTON TRANS.	TRINITY	JESUS
ben, 73	ben, 73	ben, 73	beoþ, 114, 116, 117
bilefe, 478		bileued, 478 (*for* bileueþ)	
demen, 77[9]	demen, 77	demen, 77	schulle demen (*inf.*), 79
duȝe, 475		duȝen, 475	
finde, 481			
foken, 305		foken, 305	
			forteoþ, 334
funde, 482		funden, 482	
			ibureþ, 75
		make, 389	
			wurcheþ, 398
ƿurþen, 307		ƿurþen, 307	

[8] Maidstone, 329–30, reads:
    For mani haueþ fikel muþ
    7 he is manne for-cuþ.
The second line seems to indicate that *mani* was considered a singular indefinite pronoun, equivalent to *many a man*; so *haueþ* is not included in the list of plurals.

[9] Hall and Wülcker consider *clerc* and *cniht* subjects of *demen*, present used as future, but Borgström, Schipper, and Morris regard them as objects of the infinitive *demen*. Hall, II, 297; Borgström, p. 48; Schipper, *Eng. Metrik* I, 154; Wülcker, *Beiträge* I, 256.

TEST 9

There are few present participles in the *Proverbs;* only one each in the Maidstone MS. and the Cotton transcripts. That in the Maidstone, *singinde,* 206, is Southern; but *luuiende, Sp.* 40, is Midland. The Trinity MS. contains two examples of Midland and two of Southern; the Jesus shows a ratio of 1 to 3 in favor of Southern forms.

Midland		*Southern*	
TRINITY	JESUS	TRINITY	JESUS
desiende, 253			
		liuihinde, 290	lyuyinde, 278
		lusninde, 605, 613	
singende, 206			singinde, 230
	werende, 438		wexynde, 168, 433

TEST 10

The following Midland forms of the verb *to be* are found in the Cotton transcripts and in the Maidstone and Trinity MSS:

MAIDSTONE	COTTON TRANS.	TRINITY
ben (*inf.*), 261	ben (*inf.*), 64	ben (*inf.*), 57, 64, 261, 355, 598
ben, 73	ben, 73	ben, 73
		arren, 541

None of these forms is found in the Jesus MS., which uses *beoþ* for the present indicative plural and *beon* for the infinitive.

TEST 11

The Maidstone MS. is consistently Midland in retaining the *-n* suffix of the past participle of strong verbs, and with one exception (*i-drunken,* 263), also follows the Midland custom of dropping the *i-, y-* prefix. Only one example appears in the Cotton transcripts, but that is Midland. The Trinity MS. is also Midland in the retention of *-n,* but fails to drop the *i-, y-* in three cases. In contrast, Jesus has the Southern form without *-n* in nine places out of twelve. It is completely Southern in retaining the *i-, y-,* except in compounds. The retention of both *i*- and *-n* on three occasions in both Jesus and Trinity may show some Southwestern influence.[10] The Midland character of Maidstone, Cotton, and Trinity, as against the Southern type in Jesus, is easily seen in the following table:

Midland				*Southern*	
MAIDSTONE	COT-TON	TRINITY	JESUS	MAIDSTONE COTTON TRINITY	JESUS
					a-swunde, 117
biloken, 483		biloken, 483			
					bi-swike, 116
bitoʒen, 136		bitoʒen, 136			bi-towe, 158
boren, 186					
drunken, 246		drunken, 246, 282			
for drunken, 252		for-drunken, 252			
for-ʒeten, 484		forʒeten, 484			
		forloren, 380			
		for-spu[n]ken, 352			for-swunke, 293
helden, 311		helden, 311			
					idrowe, 157
					i-dryue, 95
					i-schote, 421
sapen, 121		ascapen, 121			
sowen, 100	sopen, 100	saʒin, 100			
unborn, 243		vnboren, 243			vnbore, 449
unibeten, 244		vnbeten, 244			
vn-drunken, 246		vndrunkin, 246			
þin drunken, 282					wyn-drunke, 270
þoxen, 229		þoxin, 229			
þoxsen, 161		þoxen, 161			

[10] Wyld, *op. cit.*, p. 37.

Retention of both i- and -n

MAIDSTONE	TRINITY	JESUS
	iborin, 186	iboren, 210, 448
idrunken, 263	ydronken, 263	
		ischapen, 143
	iscoten, 456	isowen, 123

TEST 12

Maidstone, Cotton transcripts, and Trinity with relatively few exceptions[11] follow the Midland custom of retaining the *-n* of the infinitive. The Jesus MS., on the other hand, is typically Southern in showing a large majority of infinitives ending in *e* or *ie, y* or *ye*. When *-n* occurs, it is usually before a vowel, or at the end of a line.

Other indications of the localization of the manuscripts may be found in the use of certain consonants or consonant groups. *V* is often substituted for *f* in Kent and also frequently in the South and Southwest.[12] In the Jesus MS., *v* appears at times where the other MSS. keep the *f*, as for example, *Seuorde* for *Siforde*, 1; *velde* for *felde*, 169; *vouh* for *feoh*, 192; *for-vare* for *forfaren*, 222; *vere* for *fere*, 223; *bi-vore* for *biforen*, 273; *i-vo* for *ifon*, 274; *vayre* for *faire*, 347, 348. This peculiarity probably does not indicate a localization near Kent, since no examples of the Kentish change of *s + vowel* to *z + vowel* are to be found in the MS.

The Midland character of Maidstone is shown by *what* for *hwat*, 108,[13] by *fro*, 197,[14] and by *poxsen*, 161, *poxen*, 229, for O.E. *weaxen*. It also contains the Northern *sal*, as well as the usual *scal*, (79, 156), and the Northern *spilch* for the *swich*, or *swych* of the other MSS., (215, 217). Trinity has a large number of *sal* forms.

Further evidence of the Midland character of the archetype is supplied by the rimes. Lines 13 and 14 in *T.* rime *lerin, i-herin;*

---

[11] Maidstone exceptions: singe, 328, forfare, 198, sege, 215, 217, pene, 154, 318, banne, 237, laste, 476.
Cotton exceptions: samne, 34, be, *Sp.*, 57.
Trinity: samne, 34, penne, 230, banne, 237, rere, 362, liue, 476, be, 626, bisette, 633.

[12] Wyld, *op. cit.*, pp. 37, 42.

[13] O.E. *hw*, Midland *wh* and Southern *w:* Wyld, *op. cit.*, p. 50.

[14] Borgström, *op. cit.*, p. xix.

whereas in *J*. corresponding lines end in *lere, i-hure*. Since the Southern dialect of *J*. spoils the rime, it is logical to suppose that it was not the original, but that the riming Midland forms in *T*. represent the dialect of the archetype.

The above tests indicate the localization of the manuscripts as follows: Cotton and Maidstone, Southern part of East Midland; Trinity, East Midland, but even more to the Southeast; Jesus, Central South or perhaps a little to the Southwest.[15]   It has already been shown that the Jesus MS. is not authoritative.   When this is excluded, the other manuscripts agree in pointing to Southern East Midland, or the border between the Midland and the South as the locality in which the poem was originally composed.   This agreement means that the *Proverbs* can no longer be considered a purely Southern poem.   The evidence for its Midland coloring also confirms in a very satisfactory way the proof offered in a previous chapter to establish the location of Siford in Berkshire.

The precise spot at which the archetype was written cannot be determined, of course, but it would appear to belong within the limits of Berkshire, Oxfordshire, Bucks, and lower Northamptonshire.   This location would agree with the dialect characteristics, with the external evidence connecting the Maidstone MS. with Northampton, and also with the naming of Siford in the poem as the site of Alfred's gathering.

COMPARISON WITH OTHER LITERARY MONUMENTS

Something further of the position held in literature by *The Proverbs of Alfred* may be learned by comparing its linguistic forms with those of other works of the twelfth or early thirteenth centuries. I do not propose to consider purely dialectic features since the

---

[15] It seems probable that the Jesus MS. was written somewhere in the neighborhood of Hants.   It has much in common with the Egerton MS. of the *Poema Morale*, generally assigned to the Middle South, and by some scholars, particularly to Hants.   Hall (II, 292) says of *J*.: "Southern, free from South-Eastern influence.   The wavering in the representation of *a* before nasals points to the Middle South, but *ihure*, 10, *ihurd*, 205, are South-Western.   But this representation of *īe*, as well as *lyen* (*lēan*), is found in MS. *e* of the *Poema Morale*, which is generally taken as of the Middle South." This same MS. usually expresses O.E. *eo* by *eo*, also a characteristic of the Jesus MS.

Wyld tests already applied have been based on comparative study
of that type. It is my purpose here to compare forms indicating
time rather than place distinctions. I shall therefore discuss the
loss of the old diphthongs and the appearance of the new, certain
changes in consonant combinations, the loss of inflectional forms,
the introduction of foreign words, and other points particularly
indicative of certain stages of development.

The poems or prose pieces selected for comparison are: *Worcester Fragments, St. Godric's Hymn, Peterborough Chronicle, Charter of
Henry II, Vespasian Homilies, Poema Morale, Ancren Riwle, Vices
and Virtues*, Layamon's *Brut, Ormulum*, and *The Owl and the
Nightingale*. Hall, in the second volume of his *Selections from Early
Middle English*, has made a study of the phonology and accidence
of these pieces, and I have availed myself of some of his material for
comparison.

The Digraph æ

The retention of O.E. æ would make an excellent test for the age
of Early Middle English manuscripts, were it not that one must
reckon with the eccentricities of the individual scribes. Æ appears
in the *Worcester Fragments*, the archetype of which Hall (II, 232)
believes belonged to the first half of the 12th century. In *St.
Godric's Hymn*, O.E. æ is *a* except in the name *Nicholæs*. The
historian of the last part of the *Peterborough Chronicle* usually
writes O.E. ǣ as *a* and ǣ as *e*, the proper dialectic forms for that
locality, but at times he retains the old æ. This usage may be due
to the early date (*c.* 1155), but when other portions of his work are
studied, it becomes evident that the author is consciously archaic,
apparently trying as far as possible to make his contribution match
the earlier part of the chronicle. *The Charter of Henry II* is also
not typical since it was drafted on the model of an earlier charter in
which æ and other primitive forms are to be expected. In the
Vespasian Homilies the digraph is not regularly used, but appears
in a number of cases. Its retention is especially characteristic of
the Southeast.[16] In none of the manuscripts of the *Proverbs* is æ

---

[16] Hall, *op. cit.*, II, 439.

to be found.   Of the pieces which I should place after the *Proverbs*
on other grounds, the following do not contain *æ: Poema Morale*,
Lambeth MS., (the Southeast Trinity version, however, contains
three or four examples); *Ancren Riwle*, Corpus Christi and Nero
MSS., (Caius Coll. MS., one example); and *The Owl and the Nightingale*.   On the other hand, *æ* appears in the Southeastern *Vices and
Virtues*, as one would expect, although it is the exceptional rather
than the regular form.   Orm, the careful writer, represents *ēa* by
æ, and also preserves O.E. *æ* in most cases.   His work is usually
dated c. 1200, but his adoption of the classical West Saxon orthography accounts for the use of older forms.   Layamon also writes
the old *ēa* as *æ* in the *Brut*.   Like Orm, he generally keeps O.E. *æ*,
and at times even represents *ā* by *æ*.   This practice may perhaps
be due to West Saxon spelling or to an effort to preserve the atmos-
phere of the early material he is using.

The absence of *æ* in *Proverbs* manuscripts is thus not inconsistent
with its date, although some later works retain the form, as in the
Proclamation of Henry III, 1258.   It is also possible that the archetype of the *Proverbs* contained some *æ*-forms eliminated by later
scribes.

Loss of Old English Diphthongs

The diphthongs *ĕa, ĕo, ĭo, ĭe*, according to Wright,[17] became
monophthongs in the late Old English period, except in Kentish,
although they continued to be written long after the sound change
had taken place.   This statement is particularly true of *eo*, which
was long retained in the South, Southwest, and Southwest Midland.
Many *eo*-forms are found in the Jesus MS. of the *Proverbs*, although
the Southern East Midland MSS.—the Cotton transcripts, Maidstone, and Trinity—offer no examples in spite of their priority.   *Eo*-
forms are found in the *Worcester Fragments*, the *Poema Morale*
(especially MS. *e*), the *Ancren Riwle*, and Layamon's *Brut*, all pieces
from the sections partial to traditional spellings.

The very early Eastern pieces—the part of the *Peterborough
Chronicle* written c. 1155, the *Charter of Henry II*, and the *Vespasian
Homilies*—also contain some cases of the retention of *eo*, but *St.*

[17] J. and E. M. Wright, *An Elementary Middle English Grammar*, p. 29.

Godric's Hymn in Northern dialect (before 1170) does not keep the old diphthong. *Vices and Virtues*, *Ormulum*, and *The Owl and the Nightingale*, each show a few *eo*-forms.

The Old English diphthong *ea* occurs in the *Worcester Fragments*, but not in *St. Godric's Hymn*, or the portion of the *Peterborough Chronicle* under discussion. It is found in the Jesus MS. of the *Proverbs* only, and there not frequently. Layamon and Orm usually express the sound by *æ*, or if it is followed by *r* or *l* plus a consonant, either by *a* or *æ*. The other pieces listed each afford some examples, and the *Ancren Riwle*, a number, since the author regularly retains O.E. *ea*.

None of the *Proverbs* MSS. contains *ie* or *io*. In fact these diphthongs have almost entirely disappeared in the literature of the period, with the exception of *ie* in manuscripts from Kent or those under Kentish influence. The *Vespasian Homilies*, the Trinity *Poema Morale*, and *Vices and Virtues* exhibit this characteristic. The Lambeth MS. of the *Poema Morale* shows the palatalization of *e* into *ie* after *ʒ* or *g*. With a few sporadic exceptions, the diphthong *io* is not retained in any of these pieces.

Because of the use of traditional spelling in certain localities, no serious argument can be based upon the presence or absence of these Old English diphthongs. In an endeavor to find explanation for the retention of *eo* and occasional *ea* in the Jesus MS. of the *Proverbs*, I have examined the other pieces in the manuscript.[18] E. W. B. Nicholson, recent Bodley Librarian, as quoted by Miss Anna C. Paues,[19] says: "From f. 217 to the end of the volume [Jesus 29] is apparently all in one hand." I find that the scribe of this section, which includes the *Proverbs*, habitually uses *eo*-forms even when their absence in other versions of the same pieces makes one suspect that they may not have been present in the archetype. *Ea* is not so common, but examples may be found in *The Passion of our Lord*, line 246; *Poema Morale*, 65 (2), 317, 369; *Sinners Beware!* 73, 330, 333; *The Duty of Christians*, 52; *The Shires and Hundreds of Eng-*

[18] Printed by Morris in *Old English Miscellany*, E.E.T.S., orig. ser., XLIX, 37–191. For *The Owl and the Nightingale*, see Hall, *op. cit.*, I, 148.

[19] Paues, "A Newly Discovered Manuscript of the *Poema Morale*," *Anglia*, XXX (1907), 222.

land, 4, 14, 15, 20 (2), 41, 48; *The XI Pains of Hell*, 223, 256; *An Orison of Our Lady*, 11.   It seems probable, then, that the retention of *eo* and occasional *ea* in the Jesus *Proverbs* was due to the orthographic peculiarities of the Southern scribe of the second part of the manuscript.

New Diphthongs

The new diphthongs are *ei*, *au*, *ou*, *eu*, and *iu*.   The development of *ei* occurred early and is present in all of the works discussed except in *St. Godric's Hymn*, which is very short, and in *Ormulum*, where Orm's zeal for the old orthodox forms probably explains the notable exception.   *Ei* is likewise found in all manuscripts of the *Proverbs*.

Wright (p. 52), in speaking of the new diphthongs, says: "Intervocalic and final postvocalic *w* combined with the preceding vowel to form a diphthong of the -*u* type in the first half of the 12th century. . . .   The gutteral *ʒ* began to become *w* after back vowels before the end of the 12th century and then later it combined with the preceding vowel to form a diphthong of the -*u* type."

In the *Worcester Fragments*, *ou* occurs frequently; but in some cases, especially in the D fragment, the diphthong has not yet developed.   *A* + *g* is usually *aw*, but it has not yet become *au*. No cases of *eu* or *iu* occur.   *St. Godric's Hymn* contains none of these diphthongs.   In the *Peterborough Chronicle* diligent search discloses an example or two of *au*, *ou*, and *eu*, but not of *iu*.   On the whole, the *Chronicle* should not be classed among works using the new -*u* diphthongs.   The *Charter of Henry II* contains none of these combinations, but the *Vespasian Homilies* show a few cases of *eu* and *iu*, although *au* and *ou* are not represented.

The presence or absence of the -*u* diphthongs in the *Proverbs* manuscripts is indicated in the following table:

MAIDSTONE	COTTON TRANS.	TRINITY	JESUS
au			
		sa[u]lle, 33	saule, 33
		saulle, 184	
(þoh, 98)	(þoh, 98, 612)	þau, 98, 249,	(þey, 121)
		612, 615	

MAIDSTONE	COTTON TRANS.	TRINITY	JESUS
(þoh, 115, 196, 249, 295, 340)	(þoh, 340)	þauc, 295	(þeyh, 220, 311)
(þo, 113)		(þoch, 113, 196) (þocke, 340)	
	(mihten, 14)	(muȝen, 14) (muȝe, 524)	i-auhteþ, 255 mawe, 14, 403

ou

louerd, 170, 492	louerd, 28, 44, 361	louird, 28, 44, 170, 644	louerde, 28
		louerd, 361, 492, 550	louerd, 44, 177, 301
(soweth, 78)	(soþeþ, 78)	souit, 78	(soweþ, 82)
(sowen, 100)	(soþen, 89, 100)	souin, 89	(sowen, 93, iso-wen, 123)
(mowen, 79)	(moþen, 79)	mouin, 79	(mowe, 83, mo-wen, 94)
	(cnoþen, 84)	cnouen, 84	
(noht, 174, 178, 204, 296)	(noht, 105)	nout, 105, 174, 178, 628, 665	nouht, 58, 196, 201, 339
(nocht, 105)		(nocht, 441, 506)	nouhte, 383
		(noþit, 296) (þochte, 353)	(nowiht, 284)
		pouere, 397	poure, 39 pouere, 375
(dohter, 479)		douter, 479	
soule, 184	soule, 33		
	(ȝu, 29, Sp. yu)	(ȝu, 29)	ou, 29
	(ploþes, 91)	plouis, 91	plouh, 95
(ȝuþe, 127)		(aȝueþe, 127)	youhþe, 100, 106, 149
(ȝuȝþe, 135)		(ȝueþe, 135)	youþe, 157 brouhte, 266

eu

		gleu, 47, 386	(gleaw, 47) glev, 362

Maidstone	Cotton Trans.	Trinity	Jesus
		þeues, 597	vnþev, 290
		(usual	(vnþewes, 368)
		þeþes)	
		heure, 634	
	(ȝure, 28)	(ȝure, 28)	eure, 28
			lorþeu, 105
		(ȝu, 190)	eu, 214

The fact that *au, ou*, and *eu* are practically undeveloped in Maidstone or the Cotton transcripts is another indication that these manuscripts are much older than Trinity or Jesus. This in turn affords corroboration for the 12th-century date of the archetype.

Examination of the pieces in the Jesus MS. written by the *Proverbs* scribe shows that he was accustomed to the use of the new diphthongs. *Ou* and *au* are employed with practical uniformity, and *eu* appears frequently. In *The Owl and the Nightingale, Long Life, An Orison of our Lady, Doomsday, Death*, and *A Lutel Soth Sermun*, (poems which also occur in Cotton MS. Caligula A. IX), the Jesus scribe uses the diphthongs *au* and *ou*, where the Cotton MS. (of the first quarter of the 13th century[20]) gives the simple vowel. However, the J. scribe may not be entirely responsible for the new diphthongs in the *Proverbs*, since their presence in the Trinity version suggests that the forms were modernized at least to some extent before the Jesus copy.

I have not noted any examples of *iu* in the *Proverbs* MSS. It was a late development from *eu* and is practically unknown in all the pieces under discussion.[21] I shall therefore not consider it further.

In the Lambeth MS. of the *Poema Morale* instances of the use of *au* are frequent, but *ou* and *eu* have not yet appeared. The Trinity MS. of that poem, however, affords some cases of *eu*. Neither the *Brut* nor *Ormulum* contain many new diphthongs, although an occasional *au* may be found. *Vices and Virtues*, in contrast, shows a more advanced development, especially for *ou*. In the *Ancren Riwle*, at least some examples of all three diphthongs are given. The Nero MS. seems to be the most progressive in this respect.

[20] Hall, *op. cit.*, II, 450.
[21] A few cases occur in the *Vespasian* *Homilies* and at least one in *The Owl and the Nightingale.*

The archetype of the *Proverbs* belongs, then, in that period in which the old diphthongs had disappeared and the new ones were just beginning to develop. Such a period of monophthongization cannot be fixed within definite limits as is evident from the preceding discussion; but by excluding spellings from conservative sections of the country or by scribes known to be partial to traditional orthography, it is possible to place it roughly in the last third of the 12th century.

Consonant Changes

Moreover, the *Proverbs* dates before the establishment of certain consonant changes. According to Wright (p. 52), gutteral ȝ began to become *w* after back vowels before the end of the 12th century. With the exception of the *Worcester Fragments* and the *Ancren Riwle*, all[22] the pieces used for comparison exhibit this undeveloped ȝ or *g*. However, the Trinity MS. of the *Poema Morale* uses both ȝ and *w*. The Jesus MS. of *The Owl and the Nightingale* is more advanced than Cotton Caligula. The *J.* scribe regularly uses *w*, a change which may, like that in the diphthongs, be attributed to his editorship.[23] Forms in the *Proverbs* MSS. are as follows:

MAIDSTONE	COTTON TRANS.	TRINITY	JESUS
laweliche, 75	laȝelice, 70, 75	laþeliche, 70	laweliche, 72
		lauelichi, 75	lawelyche, 77
	laȝe, 8, 93	laȝe, 93	lawe, 8, 97
		laþe, 8, 557	
soriȝe, 203		soreȝe, 211, 256	seorewe, 227, 332
sorȝe, 211, 256		sorþ, 147	serewe, 235
sorwe, 123		sorþe, 203	
		seruȝe, 438	
sadel boȝe, 205		sadilboþe, 205	sadelbowe, 229
areȝe, 204, 212, 220, 221		areȝe, 204, 212, 220, 221	arewe, 228
			erewe, 236
inoȝe, 177			inowe, 199
morȝen slep, 260		morȝe-sclep, 260	

[22] *St. Godric's Hymn* affords no examples.
[23] *W* is regularly used in the other pieces in the Jesus MS. copied by this scribe.

MAIDSTONE	COTTON TRANS.	TRINITY	JESUS
		amorʒe, 251	
		moreuin, 377	
muʒe, 163, 476		moʒe, 490	
		moþe, 476	mawe, 403
		muʒe, 163, 524	mvwe, 170
oʒen, 160, 234, 494	ogen, *Sp.* 81	oʒe, 81	owe, 167, 189
oʒene, 146		oʒene, 146, 160	owere, 85
owen, 81		oþene, 234, 494	owene, 440
bitoʒen, 136		bitoʒen, 136	bi-towe, 158
		saþen, 35 (*O.E.* sagu)	
duʒeþe, 473	duʒeðe, 404	duʒeþe, 473	doweþes, 177
		duʒe, 404	
			ofer-howeþ, 445
tahte, 238		taʒte, 238	
		saʒe, 385	sawe, 361

I have not inserted in my table the following words in Maidstone in which Professor Brown[24] believes *w* was mistakenly written for *ʒ*: *chariweth*, 81, for *chariʒeth; hwungman*, 111, for *hʒungman; wyuen*, 112, for *ʒyuen; wiuen*, 117, for *ʒiuen; awen*, 124, for *aʒen*. Scribal inaccuracy in distinguishing between *þ* and *ʒ* reduces the value of this test, but it is evident from the table that the use of *w* for *g* was but little developed in Maidstone, not at all in the Cotton transcripts, partially in Trinity, and completely in Jesus. This situation again indicates the priority of the Cotton transcripts and Maidstone.

Their priority is further emphasized by inspection of the palatal *sc* as it occurs in these manuscripts. No examples of the change to *sh* are found in the Cotton transcripts, and only one in the Maidstone MS. (line 111); but in Trinity and Jesus, *sch* or *sh* is the general rule, although a few exceptions are to be found. *Sc* remains *sc* in almost all of the works of this period except *Ormulum* (*sh*), *Ancren Riwle* (*sch*), and *The Owl and the Nightingale* (generally *sch* or *sh*).

[24] "The Maidstone Text of *The Proverbs of Alfred*," *Mod. Lang. Rev.*, XXI (July, 1926), 250.

The change from *cw* to *qu* apparently took place between the composition of the *Proverbs* and the Trinity and Jesus copies. The Cotton transcripts retain *cw*,[25] but the later versions use the French *qu*. Only a few exceptional cases of *qu* may be found in the earliest pieces, but it is used consistently in the *Poema Morale* and the *Brut*, and nearly always in *The Owl and the Nightingale*, (uniformly in the Jesus text). Orm uses *qu* in Latin words, but otherwise *cw*. In *Vices and Virtues* the *cw* is preserved, and also in the *Ancren Riwle* with some exception.

Dentals

Final *d* and *þ* tend to become *t* before a word beginning with *þ*. At other times initial *þ* after a word ending in *d* or *t* is written as *t*. These assimilations became more frequent as time went on. The *Worcester Fragments* show one case: *mænet þeo* (B. 7) for *mæneþ þeo*. In *St. Godric's Hymn*, *wiþ þe* (line 4) appears without assimilation. The *Peterborough Chronicle* exhibits a number of changes from *þ* to *t* in the initial letter of the second word, as *mid te* for *mid þe*, 7 (and) *te* for *7þe*, *ðat te* or *þatte* for *þat þe*, *æt te* for *æt þe*, etc. However, there are many times when the expected assimilation does not take place. No juxtaposition of *d*, *t*, and *þ* occurs in the *Charter of King Henry*. In the *Vespasian Homilies* 7 *to* is written for 7 *þo* in line 147, and *eter* for *æt þære* in lines 13, 117.[26]

The *Proverbs* manuscripts show great variation in this point. In the Cotton transcripts initial *þ* following a final *t* or 7 has been changed to *t* in seven cases, and only three times has a possible assimilation been missed. The Maidstone MS. reads *t* for *þ* in this position twenty times out of a possible thirty-five; while Trinity affords only five examples, although the text is much longer. The T. scribe writes *it*, *et*, or *id* for *iþ* or *eþ*, as *wenit*, 317, *of-þinket*, 420, *tellit*, 628, *comit*, 235, *cumid*, 463, 531. In the examples given, the verb is followed by a word beginning with *þ* or *t*, even though it may be at the first of the next line. This circumstance gives the effect of assimilation, but since this is the general practice of the scribe, no particular importance need be attached to the fact that an

---

[25] Maidstone affords no examples. [26] Hall, *op. cit.*, I, 17.

initial *þ* follows. In the Jesus MS. there is only one assimilation: *schal-tu*, 248.

The *Poema Morale*, in both the Lambeth and Trinity MSS., shows a few instances of this change in the dentals. In *Vices and Virtues* initial *þ* becomes *t* after final *t* in the preceding word. An example of the other type of assimilation appears in line 40: *halt tin god* for *hald þin god*. Layamon, on the other hand, does not allow assimilation of dentals, but both Orm and the author of the *Ancren Riwle* use *t* for initial *þ* after *t* or *d*. The Caius MS. (p. 129, 1) reads *fondet te fordonne* for *fondið to fordonne* in the Corpus version. *The Owl and the Nightingale*, in both Cotton Caligula and Jesus texts, affords the following examples of assimilation: *dostu*, 174, 289; *axestu*, 329; *wenestu*, 219, (also *J.* 47); *speddestu*, 125; *schaltu*, 165; *wostu*, 334. To these may be added *wit þe*, *C.* 56, for *wiþ þe*.

In a discussion of the dental peculiarities of these pieces, verbs in the 3rd person singular contracted after a dental stem should also be noted. The forms in the *Worcester Fragments* are usually uncontracted, as *wendeþ*, B. 12; *scorteþ*, B. 19; *forbindeþ*, B. 42; but *met*, B. 33. In the *Vespasian Homilies* the contractions are numerous, as for example: *ett*, 163; *fett*, 42; *fet*, 171; *ȝemet*, 133; *lat*, 124; *sit*, 138. The following cases occur in the *Proverbs: pent*, *M.* 197; *wenhim* (*wen[t] him*), *T.* 197; *lat*, *Jms.* 358, *T.* 358; *let*, *J.* 298; *bi-hath*, *M.* 320; *bihait*, *T.* 320; *bi-hat*, *J.* 347; *bit*, *T.* 616; *slit*, *T.* 659. Contractions are frequent in the *Poema Morale*. Examples are: *bet*, *L.* 126, 164, *T.* 126, 166; *bit*, *L.* 126, *T.* 126, 357; *lest*, *L.* 167; *last*, *T.* 169; *sent*, *L.* 42, 46, *T.* 42; *wit*, *L.* 84, *T.* 84; *abit*, *T.* 130; *lat*, *T.* 129, 342. Only a few instances appear in *Vices and Virtues*, as *sant*, 28.[27] Contracted forms are also rare in the *Brut* and in *Ormulum*. However, *halt* occurs in line 14333 of the former, and *stannt* in line 3977 of the latter. On the other hand, the *Ancren Riwle* contains a large proportion of verbs of this type. On page 214 alone (Camden text), the following are found: *bihalt* (twice), *ethalt*, *ablent* (twice), and *understond*. Other examples are: *punt*, p. 418; *sent*, p. 424; *went*, p. 430, and more could easily be added. In *The Owl and the Nightingale* there are also a number of contractions:

---

[27] *Vices and Virtues*, E.E.T.S., orig. ser., LXXXIX, 149.

abid, 421 (*J*., *abit*); *bit*, 319 (*J*., *bid*), 323; *diht*, 399; *falt*, 37; *fiʒt*, 132; *halt*, 32; *lat*, 224 (*J*., *let*); *lust*, 168, 169; *writ*, 399.

The uncontracted singular is, of course, the more primitive form, but allowance must be made for the obvious partiality for contraction manifested in Southern pieces. However, since this peculiarity occurs at least occasionally in *Ormulum*, a Northern East Midland poem, its very limited presence in the *Proverbs* is no objection to the argument for its Midland coloring.

Inflections

It will not be of value to discuss the inflectional forms of the different literary pieces in any great detail. No real test can be based on the retention of noun and adjective declensions or traces of grammatical gender, since the practice of Southern writers was far more conservative than that in the Midland or the North. Wright (pp. 129–30) says: "Even in the O.E. period both the gender and declension of nouns fluctuated considerably in the Northumbrian as compared with the other dialects. It had almost entirely disappeared in the Midland dialects by the end of the 12th or early part of the 13th century, in the Southwestern dialects by the middle of the 13th century, and in the Southeastern dialects, including Kentish, in the latter part of the 14th century."

Thus it is not surprising to find many remnants of the old declensions in the Southeastern *Vespasian Homilies*, and *Vices and Virtues*, and in the Southern Jesus *Proverbs*, the *Poema Morale*, and *The Owl and the Nightingale*. Correspondingly scant in this respect are the *Peterborough Chronicle*, *Ormulum*, the Maidstone MS. of the *Proverbs*, and the Cotton transcripts. The manuscripts of the *Ancren Riwle* differ among themselves, apparently in accordance with the locality in which each scribe lived.

In spite of this regional divergence it may perhaps be worth while to note a few points of comparison. In almost all the works examined, the vowel of the unaccented inflectional syllable has been leveled out into *e*. In the *Worcester Fragments* some seven exceptions occur. The *Charter of Henry II*, because of its archaic model, keeps the old inflectional vowels in most cases. The *Peterborough Chronicle* retains *an* as the infinitive ending, but as a rule shows leveling elsewhere. The *Vespasian Homilies* and *Vices and Virtues* have *e*-forms for the most part, and the other pieces, including the *Proverbs*, show complete leveling.

A few of the early dual pronouns are retained in some works. These are found in the *Brut, Ormulum, The Owl and the Nightingale, Genesis and Exodus,* and *Havelok.* One example appears in the *Proverbs: unc, T.* 542.

Introduction of Foreign Words

Wright (p. 89) estimates the number of words derived from the French in literary use in England in the 12th century as only about one hundred. Between 1250 and 1350 a great many were introduced, but the earlier period is characterized by its freedom from the foreign element. The *Worcester Fragments* contain three words of French origin; *St. Godric's Hymn,* four; the *Peterborough Chronicle,* about twenty; the *Vespasian Homilies* are practically free. The *Proverbs* offer twelve; the *Poema Morale,* nine; *Vices and Virtues,* about eight. Some eighty-seven French loan-words may be found in the *Brut,* which is perhaps a small proportion when its French origin and extreme length are considered. About twenty appear in *Ormulum,* and fifty-five in *The Owl and the Nightingale;* but nearly five hundred in the *Ancren Riwle,* which also borrows heavily from the Scandinavian.[28] A rather large amount of this latter element is also found in *Ormulum,* a fact which confirms the belief that it was written in Northern East Midland. Some Scandinavian loan-words are used in the *Brut,* and a few in *The Owl and the Nightingale* and the *Peterborough Chronicle.* An occasional example appears in the other pieces.

The 12th-century position of the *Proverbs* may easily be seen in this virtual absence of foreign elements in its vocabulary.

Metre

Before summing up my conclusions, I should like to call attention to the metre of the *Proverbs.* This has been carefully studied by

[28] Hall (II, 372) argues from the Scandinavian element and other points that the archetype of the *Ancren Riwle* was Northern East Midland, and that later scribes are responsible for Southern forms.

Schipper,[29] who believes that it is the Old English alliterative line in the process of transformation into the short couplet. His views have been accepted by Skeat (pp. xxxiv ff.), Borgström (pp. lxx ff.), and others. Luick[30] has given support to this theory by finding examples of all of Sievers' five Old English metrical types in both the *Proverbs* and Layamon's *Brut*, which is similar in verse structure. In both cases the long line has been broken into two halves to form a couplet. At times rime has been introduced to bind the lines together. This is very occasional in the *Proverbs*; but more common in the *Brut*, where its increased frequency toward the end of the 32,241 lines seems to show that Layamon was gradually adopting the ideals of his original, the French *Brut* of Wace.

Schipper divides the lines in the *Proverbs* into (1) alliterative, (2) riming, (3) both alliterative and riming, and (4) four-beat verses without either rime or alliteration, occurring rarely and probably due to corruption. Alliteration takes the usual Old English form *aaax* or shows some of the old variations, as *xaaa, abab,* or *aabb,* but sometimes it is used in all four places, thus *aaaa,* in excess of the Old English method.

The *Proverbs,* in Schipper's opinion,[31] are somewhat earlier than the *Brut.* Predecessors may be recognized in such pieces as are found in the *Anglo-Saxon Chronicle* for 1036 and 1087, where the three types of lines likewise appear: those containing (1) rime only, (2) alliteration only, (3) a combination of both.

The *Worcester Fragments* illustrate the alliterative long line with an occasional middle rime. These could easily be broken up into verses similar to those in the *Proverbs.* *St. Godric's Hymn* is based on a Latin model, and the *Poema Morale* uses the septenary, likewise derived from the Latin. This is its first use in England, and it is much less regular than in *Ormulum,* where it has been handled with conscientious regard for uniformity. *The Owl and the Nightingale* is written in short rimed couplets, based on the French model, but skillfully varied at the pleasure of the author.

---

[29] Schipper, *Englische Metrik,* I, 146 ff. *History of English Versification* (translation of an abridged version of the above), p. 67 ff.
[30] Luick, "Geschichte der Heimischen Versarten," Paul's *Grundriss der Germanischen Philologie,* 2nd ed., II, part 2, pp. 143–153.
[31] *History of English Versification,* p. 74.

From this survey, it is evident that the crude and transitional metrical form of the *Proverbs* places it early in the list of Middle English poems. It is added proof for the twelfth-century date.

In the course of these chapters I have endeavored to show that *The Proverbs of Alfred* cannot be dated later than the 12th century because (1) quotation by Layamon in the *Brut* fixes the *terminus ad quem* at 1205; (2) reminiscences are also found in the 12th-century *Lambeth Homilies;* (3) the almost complete lack of the new -*u* diphthongs in the older manuscripts indicates a 12th-century date; (4) this is further evidenced by the retention of *sc, cw,* and gutteral ȝ following a back vowel; (5) foreign loan-words have scarcely begun to be introduced; (6) the metre is of an early and transitional character. I have also given reasons to prove that the *Siford* of the *Proverbs* is Siford in Berkshire. The fact that the form used is the same as that found in *Domesday Book* supports the argument that the *Proverbs* was composed in an early period. By means of linguistic tests I have established the Midland coloring of the original poem. This combined with the identification of *Siford* as Siford, Berks, enables me to locate the home of the archetype as somewhere near the border of the East Midland and the South. Thus the conclusion to which this investigation has brought us coincides fully with the paleographical opinion expressed by Wanley, the only scholar to leave a first-hand description of the Cotton Galba MS. I believe with him that it was written "circa temp. Henrici II. aut Ricardi I." Although there may have been some foundation for these *Proverbs* in lost Anglo-Saxon material, yet the archetype of the existing text of the *Proverbs* cannot antedate Cotton Galba to any great extent. It is even possible that the Cotton MS. was actually the archetype. In either case I believe that the original of *The Proverbs of Alfred* may be dated as early as the third quarter of the twelfth century.

PARALLEL TEXT

THE ARRANGEMENT OF THE TEXT

IN THE left-hand column, lines 1–30 consist of the careful transcript made by Wanley from the remaining fragment of Cotton Galba MS. A. XIX, printed by him in Hickes's *Thesaurus*, III, 231. The Cotton Galba MS. may be regarded as the archetypal MS. of the *Proverbs*. Even this fragment has been destroyed since Wanley's time.

Lines 31–71 are taken from Hearne's transcript of Spelman's *Life of Alfred the Great* as prepared for the press. This transcript, now preserved in the Bodleian Library (MS. Rawlinson D. 324), is even more authentic than that in the printed *Life of Alfred* (1709). For his text of the *Proverbs* Spelman used a copy made from the Cotton Galba MS. by Sir Thomas Cotton early in the 17th century. The extracts from Spelman's text have been copied for me from the Rawlinson MS. by Miss E. G. Parker of Oxford.

Beginning with line 72, I give the selections from the *Proverbs* preserved in the Maidstone MS. (which begins at that point) and recently printed by Professor Carleton Brown in the *Modern Language Review*, XXI (July, 1926), 252–55. The text as there printed I have collated with a photograph of the original. The manuscript at Maidstone, although the earliest of the extant MSS., does not give the complete text of the *Proverbs* but only selections, under the title *Dicta Alfredi*. The gaps between the selections preserved in the Maidstone MS. have been filled by adding, under proper designation, the corresponding lines from Trinity College Camb. MS. 323 (B. 14.39), which I have compared with the rotograph of the manuscript in the Library of Congress.

In this way a complete text of the *Proverbs* has been made up which in each of its sections offers the most authoritative representative of the archetype.

For comparison with this text I have added in the right-hand column a transcript of 119 lines of the poem made in the early 17th century by Richard James, from a copy of the *Proverbs* by Thomas

Allen, believed to be from the MS. in the Cotton Library. The James version (MS. Jms. 6 in the Bodleian Library) was printed by Professor Carleton Brown in the *Modern Language Review*, XXI (July, 1926), 256–7.

Since the full Trinity and Jesus texts are accessible in several editions, I have not thought it necessary to reprint them here. Skeat's *Proverbs of Alfred* or Borgström's book of the same title may be used as a supplement. The Borgström text, although less available in this country, is more convenient, since the line numbers in his edition follow the order of the Trinity MS.

I have used this numbering in the present text.

Wanley		*James*
(1)		(1)
At Sifforde seten		At sifforde
þeines manie		seten þeines manie,
fele Biscopes		fele biscopes,
fele Boc-lered	4	fele boclered.
Erles prude		erles prude.
Cnihtes egleche		7 cnihtes egleche.
þer þas Erl Alfrich		þer þas erle alfrich
of þe Lage spuðe þis	8	of þe laʒe spuðe þis.
ec Alfrede		7 ec alfrede
Enʒle hirde		enʒle hirde.
Enʒle derlinʒ		enʒle derlinʒ.
On Enʒelonde he þas Kinʒ	12	on Enʒlond he þas kinʒ.
hem he ʒan laren		hem he ʒan leren.
spo hi heren mihten		spo hi heren mihten.
hu hi here lif		hu hi here lif
leden scolden	16	leden scolden.
Alfred he þas on Enʒelond		Alfred he þas on onʒelond
a Kinʒ þel spiðe stronʒ		a kinʒ þel spiðe stronʒ.
he þas Kinʒ and Clerc		he þas kinʒ 7 clerc.
þel he luuede Godes þerc	20	þel he luvede ʒodes þerc.

13. *Laren*, error for *leren*. *Jms.* and *Sp.*, *leren*; *T.*, *lerin*; *J.*, *lere*. O. Eng.

lǣran became *leren* or *lere* in Midland and Southern dialects of M. English.

he þas þise on his þord	he þas þise on his þorde.
and þar on his speche	7 þare on his speche.
he þas þe þisest man	he þas þe þiseste man
þat þas on Enʒelond on. 24	þat þas on Enʒelond.

(2)

Ðus cþað Alured	þus cþað Alured
Enʒle frofre	enʒle frofre.
þolde ʒe nu liþen	þolde ʒe nu liþen
and lusten ʒure Louerd 28	7 lusten ʒure louerd
7 he ʒu þolde þisen	7 he ʒu þolde þisen
þisliche þinʒes.	þisliche þinges

Spelman

Hu ye michten werlds	hu ʒe mihten þerldes
wurthecipe welden, 32	þurðscipe þelden
And ec yure soule	7 ec ʒure soule
samne to Criste.	samne to Criste
Wise weren the cwethen	

24. *Jms.* and *Sp.* omit the final *on*, but it is retained by *T.* and *J.*, a fact which seems to indicate that it was present in the archetype. An intelligent transcriber, such as Thomas Allen or Sir Thomas Cotton, James, or even Spelman, might easily omit the superfluous word. Professor Carleton Brown has suggested that the second *on* may not be the preposition, but "unus," although the syntax is unusual.

31. Spelman's transcript is arranged in long lines, sometimes without regard for the termination of the original verses. I have broken these lines up into the usual short verse form.

Hall (II, 286) speaks of considerable differences between the three versions of Spelman: Hearne's transcript in Rawlinson D. 324, the *Life* in English published in 1709, and the Latin translation of the *Life* published in 1678. I have compared the Rawlinson text with the printed *Life* of 1709 and find in the parts directly quoted from the *Proverbs* only seven slight variations:

		RAWLINSON	LIFE
line	4	*swuthwise*	*swuth wise*
"	9	*luvied*	*luuied*
"	15	*michten*	*mihten*
"	35	*lagelich*	*lagelic*
"	36	*cniht*	*cnith*
"	41	*nor*	*or*
"	42	*te*	*the*

Since the Rawlinson long line numbers do not correspond to those of my text, I shall therefore call attention in the notes to any of the variations occurring in the selections used. For *michten*, line 31, the *Life* of 1709 reads *mihten*.

the saide the King Alfred.   36
Mildeliche I mune yu
mine dere frend,
arme And edi
lede, luuiende   40
that ye all drede   Alle dreden
yure Drihten Crist,   ʒure drihten criste
luuiend him and licen.
for he is Louerd of Lif.   44
he is one God
ouer all Godnesse.

. . . .

. . . .   48
He is one blisse
ouer alle blessedness.
He is one manne,
milde maister.   52
he one folce
fader, And frofre.
he is one riht wis
and riche King,   56
That him ne scal be pane
noht of his will
Hwo him here on werlde
wurthend and eth.   60

39. MS., *edilede*. Read *edi*[*e*], *lede lu-uiende*.

43. Read *luuien* for *luuiend*.

47–8. These lines are omitted according to the Trinity and Jesus MSS. *J.* reads:

> He is one gleaw
> ouer alle glednesse.

T. fails to keep the balanced structure, probably because of corruption:

> 7 he is gleu
> ouer alle glade þinhes.

52. *T.* and *J.* use the superlative: *T.*, *mildist*; *J.*, *mildest*.

53. *T.* and *J.* read, "He is one folkes."

56. *T.* and *J.* read, "And so (*T.*, suo) riche king." The *so* is useful in introducing the following result clause.

57. Read *pane* for *pane*.

60. "Wurthend and eth" is unintelligible. Skeat suggests "wurþen ðenkeþ." This interpretation is supported by the readings of the other MSS.: *T.*, "þrþin þenket"; *J.*, "wrþie þencheþ."

(3)

Thus cwath Aluerd
engle frofre.

He mai no riht cing   Ne mai no riht cinȝ
ben under Crist self,   64   ben under criste self
But he be boc-lered,   bute he be boclered
and wis o loage,   65*   and þis o loare
And he hise writes wel   he his þittes þel icþeme
    icweme,
and he cunne Letres   7 he cunne lettres
locen him selue   68   locen himselfe
hu he scal his lond   hu he scall his lond
Laȝelice helden.   laȝelice helden

(4)

Thus cwath Aluerd,
engle frofre.   71*

Maidstone

þe erl and þe aþeling   72   þe erl 7 þe aþelinȝ
þe ben under þe king   þo ben under þe cinȝ
þat lond to leden   þe lond to leden
mid laweliche deden   mid laȝelice deden
boþe þe clerc an te cniht   76   boðe þe clerc 7 þe cniht
Demen euenliche riht   demen euenliche riht
for after þat þe man soweth   for after þat te man soþeþ
þar after he sal mowen   þer after he scall moþen
and efrilches mannes dom   80
to his owen dure chariweth.

65*. "and þis o loare (*Sp.*, loage)" is
    omitted in *T.* and *J.*
66. *T.* supports *Sp.* with *prites*, although
    the *r* has been written in above the
    line. *J.* reads:
            and he his wyttes
            swiþe wel kunne.
    T. gives *kenne* for *icweme* (please), a
    verb which certainly does not fit.

Perhaps it is a corruption for *icunne*,
as Skeat suggests in his glossary. If
the reading *þittes* of James is to be
retained, neither *icweme* nor *icunne*
is satisfactory. Perhaps *icweme* is a
corruption of some form of *cwician*,
to quicken or cultivate.
71*. *engle frofre* omitted in *T.* and *J.*
81. The Maidstone scribe has occasion-

Spelman

(5)

Thus cwath Aluerd.		þe cniht bihoueð
the cniht behoveth		ceneliche to cnopen
Ceneliche to mowen	84	uor to perie þe lond
nor to werce the lond,		of hunʒer 7 of herezonʒ
Hunger, and of heregong,		þat te churche haue ʒriþ
that te chureche haue Grith,		7 te cherl be in friþ
and te cherl be in frith,	88	hise sedes to sopen
His sedes to sowen,		his medes to mopen
hise medes to mowen,		his plopes to driuen
His Plowes to driven		to ure alre bilif
to ure alre bilif.	92	þis is þe knihtes laʒe
This is the cnihtes lage		to locen þat it pel fare
to locen that it wel fare.		

Maidstone

(6)   (6)

. . . .

Wih-vten wisdom	96	piðuten pisdom
is wele un-wurh		is pelðe pel unpurð
for þoh man hauede		for þoh o man ahte
hundt seuenti akeres		hunt-seuenti aceres
an hes hauede sowen	100	7 hes hauede sopen
al mid rede golde		al mid rede ʒolde
And te glod grewe		7 te ʒold ʒrepe
so gras doþ on erþe		spo ʒras doð on erðe

ally written *w* for ʒ, probably on
account of confusing *p* with ʒ in his
copy.

owen, error for *oʒen; chariweth* for
chariʒeth.

82–94. This is the last section directly
quoted by Spelman. He next pro-
ceeds to a translation of the first
94 lines "according to our more current English," and concludes with
a looser paraphrase of six of the
later divisions.

84. Spelman's *mowen* is doubtless an
error. *Jms.* and *T.* read *cnopen,* and
J. paraphrases "kenliche on to
fone," boldly to undertake.

85. Spelman's *nor* should be *uor.* See
Jms. The *Life* of 1709 reads *or.*
Spelman probably copied *werce* for
werie. T. and *J.* support *Jms.*

87. The *Life* of 1709 reads *the* for *te.*

95. *T.,* "þus quad helfred."

102. *glod,* error for *gold.*

Ne were his wele   104   ne þere his þelðe
nocht þe wurhere   noht þurþ
bute he him of fremde   but he hime of fremðe
frend iwerche   frende iþurche.
for what is gold bute ston   108   uor hþat is gold but ston.
Bute it hafe wis man.   bute it haue þis man.

(7)

. . . .

Sholde nefre hwungman
wyuen him to iuele   112
þo him hise wise
wel ne like
Ne þoh he ne welde
at þat he wolde   116
for crist mai wiuen
þanne he wule
god after iuele
weleþe after wrakesih   120
wel is him þath sapen is.

(8)

. . . .

Sorwe hit is to rowen
awen þe se-flode   124

105. *T., wrþere.*
106. The Maidstone reading, *fremde*, is
supported by Spelman's paraphrase,
"unless that of an Enemy one could
make it become his Friend." Trinity reads *fremede*, but *J., frumþe*,
a probable corruption. See Skeat,
p. 56, for an example of the confusion of *frymðe* and *fremde.*
110. *T.*, "þus qu*ad* alfred."
111. *M., hwungman* for *hʒungman.* Spelman's paraphrase reads, "A young
man must never give himself to
Evil."
112. *M., wyuen* for *ʒyuen.*
116. *T.* and *J.* read *al* for *at.* Spelman's

paraphrase supports *al:* "nor
though he enjoys not everything
he would."
117. *T.* and *J.* read *god*, but *M*'s *crist* is
supported by Spelman's *Christus.*
The *M.* scribe wrote *wiuen* for
ʒiuen.
121. *M*'s reading, *sapen*, is closer to that
of *J.* (*ischapen is*), and Spelman
("he that is made for it"), than it is
to *T.* (*mot ascapen*).
122. *T.*, "[þ]us qu*ad* alfred."
123. Elsewhere *M.* reads *sorge* or *sorige.*
This is perhaps another case of
confusing *þ* and *ʒ.*
124. *Awen* for *aʒen.*

so it is to Swinken
aȝenes vniselþe
ac wel is him on ȝuþe
þe swinch was iȝiuene   128
her on werlde
wele to winnen
And he muȝe in elde
ednesse helden   132
And he m[id] is welþe
wirche godes wulle
þanne is his ȝuȝþe
swiþe wel bitoȝen.   136

(9)

· · · · · · · · ·

Ȝif þu hauest welþe
in þisse werlde
ne gin þu nefre for-þi   140
al to wlonc wurþen
for ahte nis non eldere stren
ac is godes lone
þanne it is his wille   144
þer fro we sullen wenden
and ure oȝene lif
mid alle forþ leten

128. A difficult line in all manuscripts.
T. reads "þe suinch ƿas yanen" or
ẏauen (altered to ẏapen in later
ink; see Borgström's note). J. paraphrases loosely:
  þe mon þe on his youhþe
  swo swinkeþ.
M. clears up the verb by the reading
iȝiuene, which the T. scribe may
have copied as ẏauen. M's swinch
is perhaps correct as it stands:
"well is it for him who in youth was
given the task of winning wealth
here in the world." However the
ironic use of swinch (swink, labor,

toil) seems strained. Swinch may
be an error for swich: "well is it for
him such as (who) was given to win
wealth. . . ." Since M. and T.
agree so closely, I suggest that the
archetype itself may have contained the error of swinch for swich
caused by the eye catching the
word swinken three lines above.
The mistake might also be explained by an elongated dot over
the i in swich which was inter-
preted by some scribe as the ab-
breviation for n.

137. T., "[þ]us quad alfred."

þanne sullen ure fon   148
to ure fe gripen
welden ure madmes
and liten vs bi-menen.

(10)

. . . .   152
Mani man þeneþh
þath he þene ne þarf
longes liues
and him sal liȝen þe þrench   156
For þanne he his lif
alre best luueþ
þanne scal he leten
lif his oȝen   160
Nis no þurt þoxsen
in þude ne in felde
þat efre muȝe þe feiȝe
fere up-helden   164
Not no man þe time
hþanne he scal henne rimen
ne no man þe ende
hþanne he scal heþen þen-   168
    den
Drichtin hit one þot
domes louerd
hþanne þe ure lif
leten scullen.   172

151. *T.* reads "lutil us bimenen"; *J.*,
    "and leten vs by-hinde." The
    archetypal MS. may have con-
    tained the form *lite*, little. Some
    careless stroke in an early MS. was
    perhaps read by the copyist as the
    abbreviation for *n.* It seems more
    probable that *liten* is an error for
    litel than that it represents *leten*,
    especially since *bi-menen* would then
    have to be read intransitively: "let
    us lament." No example of an
    intransitive use of this word earlier
    than 1305 is given in the *N.E.D.*
164. *fere*, from O.E. *feorh*, life. *T.*
    reads "þe lif up-helden"; the scribe
    of *J.* has not understood the old
    word and so has written "furþ
    vp-holde." The proper form for
    the Midland dialect would have
    been *ferh* (O.E. *eo<e*).
169. *Drichtin* is an unusual spelling.
    Line 180, *Drihten.*

(11)

.   .   .   .   173
Lef þu þe noht to spiþe
uppe þe se flode
If þu hauest madmes manie   176
and inoȝe gold ⁊ siluer
it scal purþen to noht
to duste it scal driuen
Drihten scal lifen efre   180
⁊ mani man for his gold
haueþh godes erre
⁊ þurh his siluer
his soule he for-leseþ   184
Betere him bicome
boren þat he ne ꝑere.

Trinity

(12)

[þ]us qᵤad alfred
lustlike lust me   188
lef dere
⁊ ich her ȝu ꝑille leren
ꝑenes mine
ꝑit ⁊ ꝑisdome   192

Maidstone

Ƿisdom alle ꝑele ouergoþ   193
Siker he mai sitten
hꝑo him mide sendeþ
for þoh his ꝑele him at-go   196
his ꝑit ne ꝑent him nefre fro
Ne mai he nefre for-fare

185. *J.* supports this reading with *by-come*. *T.* reads "betere him were."
191. *ꝑenes*, error for *ꝑines*.

193. Compare Trinity, lines 192–3.
198. MS., *neuefre*, with dots under *ue* for deletion.

hƿo him to fere haueþ
hƿiles þat his lif 200
lasten mote.

(13)

. . . .

if þu hauest soriȝe
seiȝe þu it noht þe areȝe 204
Seie it þine sadel boȝe
7 rid te singinde
þanne seiþ þe man
þath þine ƿise ne can 208
þat te þine ƿise
ƿel likeþ
Sorȝe if þu hauest
7 te areȝe it seist 212
bi foren he þ[e] bimeneþ
bihinden he þe biteleþ
þu it miht sege sƿilch man
þat it te ful ƿuel an 216
Sƿilch man þu mith sege þi
sor
he ƿolde þat tu hauedest mor
for-hidet in þin herte stille
for-helet ƿiþ þe areȝe 220
let tu nefre þe ar[e]ȝe ƿiten
al þat þe ne likeþ.

214. Supported by *J.*, *tele*. *T.* reads
scarned.
217. *mith* for *miht*—accidental meta-
thesis.
219. *M.* clears up the meaning of this
line. Evidently the scribes of *T.*
and *J.* both found it hard to read.
The former tried to copy what he
saw and wrote *forþi hit*. The
latter characteristically used his
own words to express the sense he
gathered—"By-hud hit."
    For-hidet, *M.* 219, and *for-helet*,
M. 220, represent *for-hide it* and *for-
hele it*. See *T.* 220, *for-hele hit*.
222. *T.* and *J.* are closer here than either
of them is to *M.* *T.* reads "al
þat þin herte þenket"; *J.*, "al þat
þin heorte by-wite."

(14)

. . . .

Þis child is fader blisse   224
if it so bitideþ
þat tu bern ƿeldest
hƿiles it his litel
ler hit mannes þeƿes   228
þanne it is ƿoxen
it scal ƿenden þer-to
þanne scal þi bern
þas þe beth ƿurþen   232
7 if þu letest him ƿelden
al ƿille his oȝen
þanne he cumeþ to elde
sore it scal him reƿen   236
7 me scal banne þe ƿit
þat him furst tahte
þanne scal þi bern
þi bode ouergangen   240
betere þe ƿere
bern þat tu nahtest

224. For the different versions of this paragraph, printed in parallel columns, see p. 18, *supra*. Since the Spelman paraphrase supports the Maidstone and Trinity versions very closely, I shall quote this section from the paraphrase in full.

"Thus quoth Alfred: A wise Child is the Blessing of his Father. If thou hast a Child, while it is yet but little, teach it the Precepts that belong to a Man, and when it is grown up it will follow them; then shall thy Child become such as shall recompense thee: but if thou lettest him go after his own Will, when he cometh to age it will grieve him sore, and he shall curse him that had the tuition of him: then shall thy Child transgress thy Admonition, and it would be better for thee that thou hadst no Child; for a Child unborn is better than one unbeaten."

226. *J*. supports *M*. with *bern; T*. reads *chil[d]. T., ƿeldest; J., ibidest*.

231. At this point *J*. begins to paraphrase freely and insert lines. *T*. supports *M*. closely, but uses *child* for *bern* in this line and elsewhere in the paragraph.

234. *T*. and *J*. place *owene* before *wille*.

236. *J*. uses this thought to conclude the paragraph, thus violating the original order as established by *M., T.*, and the Spelman paraphrase.

238. *T*. preserves the earlier *taȝte*.

240. *T., forbod; J., ibod*.

for betere is bern unborn
þanne unibeten. 244

(15)

. . . .
Drunken 7 vn-drunken
efre is ƿisdom ƿel god
þarf noman drinken þe lasse 248
þoh he be ƿiþ ale ƿis
Ac he þat drinkeþ
7 disiȝeþ þer among
So þat he for drunken 252
Desiȝeþ him ƿurcheþ
He scal ligen ale niht
litel scal he slepen
Him suhþ sorȝe to 256
so doþ salt on flesce
sukeþ þur his liche
so doþ leche blod
7 his morȝen slep 260
scal ben mucheles þe ƿersse
hƿo so on euen
iuele haueþ idrunken.

Trinity

(16)

Þus quad alfred 264
Ne salt þu þi ƿif   ne ȝin þu nefre þi ƿif
bi hire ƿlite chesen   bir hire ƿlite chesen.
Ne for non athte   ne uor non ehte
to þine bury bringen 268   to þi buri brinȝen.
her þu hire costes cuþe
for moni mon for athte

244. *J.* writes *vnbuhsum* against the authority of *M.*, *T.*, and the Spelman paraphrase.
249. *T.* reads *ƿid ale.* Borgström translates *with ale;* Skeat, *withal.*
251. *T.*, *amorȝe.*

253. *T.*, *desiende.*
254. *ale* for *alle.*
267, 270. *athte* for *ahte.*
269. *her* for *er.* The *T.* scribe frequently prefixes an *h*, as "þe herl 7 þe heþeling," (line 72).

iuele ihasted
7 ofte mon on faire   272
fokel chesed
þo is him þat iuel þif   þo is him þ ifel þif
brinhit to is cotlif   brinȝeð to his cot lif
so his oliue   276
þat iuele þiued
for he sal him often
dreri maken.

(17)

Þus quad alfred: 280

Maidstone

þur-þu nefre so þod   281
ne so þin drunken
þat efre seiȝe þu þi þif
al þat is ille   284
For þoh hoe seȝe þe bi-foren
þine fon alle
7 tu hire mid þorde
þraþþed hauedest   288
hoe ne scolde it leten
for þinge
þat ho ne scolde þe up-Breiden
of þine bale-siþes   292
for þimman is þord-þod

271. Probably *ihasted* represents *i-ahteþ* from O. E. *ge-eahtian*, to estimate or value. The *T.* scribe's use of *h* and the substitution of *st* for *ht* would account for the form. Compare *J.*:

> For mony mon for ayhte
> vuele i-auhteþ.

Also compare *Laws of Alfred*, 26.

274–5. Maidstone contains these two lines. They are placed at the end of the MS. and read:

> þo is him þat iuel þif
> Bringeþ to is cot lif.

276. *J.* reads "So him is alyue."

284. *T.* reads "al þat þi þille be"; *J.*, "alle þine wille." However *M*'s line is possible. Advice not to tell everything that is ill or going wrong is consistent with the use of *bale-siþes* (292).

290. *T.* completes the line with *liuihinde*; *J.*, *lyuyinde*.

7 haueþ tunge to spift
þoh hoe þel þolde
ne mei hoe noht þiþ-helden.　296

(18)

. . . .

þur-þu nefre so þod
ne so dusi o þi mod
þat efre seiȝe þu þi frond　300
al þat te ne likeþ
ne alle þe þonkes
þat tu þoht hauest
for ofte sibbe men　304
foken hem bi-tþenen
7 if so bi-tideþ
proþe þat ȝe þurþen
þanne þot þin oȝe fend　308
þat er þiste þi frend
betere þe bicome
þi þord þere helden
for hþanne muþ maþeleþ　312
more þanne he scolde
þanne scollen his eren
eft it iheren.

(19)

. . . .　316

Mani man þeneþ
þat he þene ne þarf
frend þat he habbe
þer me him faire bi-hath　320
seȝeþ him faire bi-fore
7 fokel attende

296. *T.*, "noþit þelden"; *J.*, "nowiht welde."
312. The *T.* scribe did not recognize this archaism (< O.E. *maðelian*) and wrote *mamelit.*

320, 323. *J.* supports *me.* *T.* reads *mon.*
322. *T.* supports *fokel attende,* but uses *h* before *e* (M.S. *at-hénden*). *J.* paraphrases: "and frakele bi-hynde."

So me mai þe loþe
lengest leden   324
Gin þu nefre leuen
alle mannes speche
ne alle þe þinges
þat tu herest singe   328
For mani haueþ fikel muþ
7 he is manne for-cuþ
Scal he þe neuere cuþen
Hƿanne he þe bi-spiken.   332

(20)   (20)

. . . .

Mani appel is uten *grene*   mani appel is uten grene.
briht on beme   7 brihte on beme:
7 biter þiþ-innen   336   7 bitter þiðinnen.
So is manni þimman   so is mani þimman
in hire fader bure   in hire fader bure.
scene under scete   scene under scete.
7 þoh hoe is scondes ful   340   7 þoh he is scondes full

. . . .

So is mani gadelig
godeliche on horse

323. *J.* reads *loþe;* but *T., þelþe,* which
   seems irrelevant and may have been
   a misunderstanding for *þe loþe*
   written close enough to suggest one
   word in the copy.
324. *J.* supports *leden;* but *T.* writes
   helden since *leden* is impossible with
   his reading *þelþe* in the previous
   line. However the manuscript
   looks as if the word had originally
   been *leden.* The *l* before the *d* is
   faint and apparently inserted, and
   the *h* appears to me to be a doc-
   tored *l.*
330. *J., for-cuþ; T., cuð.*
331. Supported by *J.,* "Nele he þe
   cuþe." *T.* reads, "ne saltu neuere

kneþen." The long *s* of *saltu* has
   been crossed by mistake.
332. *J.,* "wule bi-kache"; *T.,* "þole
   bikechen."
334. *T.* reads *þid-uten* for *uten. J.* con-
   denses three lines into two:
      Mony appel is bryht wiþ-vte
      and Bitter wiþ-inne.
335. *T., leme.*
338. *J.* supports *fader. T.* has misread
   the word as *faire.*
341. *T.* offers a unique line: "in an
   stondes þile."
342. *gadelig* for *gadeling* (*T.*). *J.* reads
   gedelyng, the proper form for the
   Southern dialect.

ƿlonc op his stede   344
and un-ƿurþ at þe nude.

Trinity
(21)

Þus quad alureid
Idilscipe 7 orgul prude
þat lerit ȝung ƿif   348
leþere þeƿes
7 often to þenchen
don þat he ne scolde
ȝif he for spuken spoti ƿuere   352
sƿo hie ne þochte
ac þoch hit is iuel to beþen
þat ter ben ne ƿille
for ofte mused þe catt   356
after þe moder

ƿose lat is ƿif   hƿo so lat his ƿif
his maister ƿurþen   his master ƿurden.
[ne] sal he neuer ben   360   ne scal he nefre ben
is ƿordes louerd   his ƿordes louerd
ac he sal him rere dreiȝe
7 moni tene selliche haƿen
Selden sal he ben on sele.   364

344. *T.*, *perȝe*, which Borgström believes is *werwe* (*werue*), steed. Compare *Old Eng. Hom.* I, 85. *J.* reads "bi þe glede," possibly on account of a misreading of *stede* in some early copy.
345. *J.* supports *nude* with *neode*. *T.* reads *on ƿike*.
346. MS., *aluid* with stroke over *u*.
347. *J.*, *ouer-prute*.
349. *J.*, *vuele* for *leþere*.
351. *J.* inserts two lines:
        þene vnþeƿ lihte
        leten heo myhte.

352. Read *for-swunken swoti were* (Skeat and Borgström).
355. Skeat reads *trewe* for *ter* on the analogy of *J.*: "þat beo nule treowe." Borgström suggests *tre*, tree.
358. The James text explains the following four lines of Trinity, which are somewhat confused by the use of *ƿose* (358) for *hƿo so*, *is* (358, 361) for *his*, and the omission of *ne* (360).
362. *J.* adds these lines:
        Ac heo hine schal steorne
        to-trayen and to-teóne
        And selde wurþ he blyþe and gled
        þe mon þat is his wiues qued.

(22)

Þus q*u*ad alfreud
ȝif þu frend bi-ȝete
mid þi fre biȝete
loke þat þu him þeine   368
mid alle þeuues þines
loke þat he þe be mide
bi-foren 7 bi-hinden
þe bett he sal þe reden   372
at alle þine neden
7 on him þu maist þe tresten.
ȝif is troþþe deȝh
ac ȝif þu hauist a frend to day   376
7 to moreuin dr*i*uist him awei
þenne bes þu one
al so þu her þere
7 þanne is þi fe forlore*n*   380
7 þi frend boþen
betere þe bicome
frend þat þu neþedest.

(23)

Þus q*u*ad alfred   384
þurch saȝe mon is þis
7 þurch selþe mon is gleu
þurch lesin[ge] mon is loð
7   þuruh   luþere   þrenches   388
    vnþurþ
7 hokede honden make þen
    mon
is heþit to lesen

---

365. This section is unique in Trinity.
       Alfreud is written with a stroke
       over the *u*.
369. *þines* for *þine*. The *s* was probably
       added under the influence of the

preceding word *þeuues*.
375. MS., *þif; troÿþe*.
379. *her* for *er*.
387. The letters after *lesin* have been
       cut away. *J.* reads *lesinge*.

ler þu þe neuer
ouer-mukil to leþen   392
ac loke þine nexte
he is ate nede god
7 freɳdchipe oƿerlde
farrest[u] to þurchen   396
ƿid pouere 7 ƿid riche
ƿid alle men iliche
þanne maist þu sikerliche
seli sittiɳ   400
7 faren ouer londe
hƿar so bet þi ƿille.

(24)

þus qᴜɑd aluᵣed
ȝif þu hauist duȝe   404
7 drichen þe senden
Ne þeng þu neuere þi lif
to narruliche leden
Ne þine faires   408
to faste holden
for ƿer hachte is hid
þer is armþe inoch
7 siker ich it te saiȝe   412
letet ȝif þe liket
spich mon mai aftᵉʳ þe

if þu hauest duȝeðe.
7 drihten it te sendeþ
ne ȝin þu nefre þi lif
to narƿlice leden.
ne þine faires
to faste helden.
for þere ehte is ihud.
þer is soreȝe inoh.
sicer ic it te seȝȝe.
lef it if þe liceð.
spulc man mai after þe

391. *J.* expands at this point:
    From lesynge þu þe wune,
    And alle vnþewes þu þe bi-schune;
    so myht þu on þeode
    leof beon in alle leode.
392. *leþen,* error for *leȝen.*
395. *J.* reads:
    At chepynge and at chyreche
    freond þu þe iwurche.
396. The first word of this line is difficult
    to read. Skeat and Kemble be-
    lieved it was *fairest.* Borgström is
    undecided between *farrest* and
    fairest, but thinks the thought best

brought out by *farrest*[*u*]. He
suggests that the *u* may have been
dropped on account of the duplica-
tion of the sound (*tu to*). After
inspecting the rotograph, I am in-
clined to Borgström's opinion. The
fact that the letter is not dotted
strengthens the case.
402. *bet* for *beþ.* The *T.* scribe fre-
    quently writes *t* for *þ.*
404. *T., duȝe* for *duȝeþe.*
405. *T., senden* for *sende* or *sendeþ.*
    Compare James.
406. *T., þeng* for *þenk.*

þi god ƿelden
ofte binnen þine burie   416
bliþe ƿenden
þad he ne ƿele heren
mid muþe moneȝen
ac euuere him of-þinket   420
þen he [of] þe þenked.

þi ƿelðe ƿelden.
ofte binne þi buri
bliðe sitten.
þ̵ te ne ƿile heren
mid muðe muniȝen.
ac efre him ofþincheþ
panne he of þe þencheþ.

(25)

þus qu*a*d alu*r*ed
Vretu noth to sƿiþe
þe ƿord of þine ƿiue   424
for þanne hue bed ipraþed
mid ƿordes oþer mid dedes
ƿimmo*n* ƿeped for mod
oft*er* þa*n*ne for eni god   428
7 ofte lude 7 stille
for to ƿurchen hire ƿille
Hue ƿeped oþer-ƿile
þen hue þe ƿille biƿilen   432
Salo*m*on hid haƿit isait
Hue can moni yuel reid.
Hue ne mai hit non oþir don
for ƿel he*r*liche hue hit bigan   436
þe mo*n* þad hire red foleƿid
he bringeþ him to seruȝe

418. T., *he* for *þe*. Compare James.
421. *Of* is lacking in the Trinity MS.
423. *Vretu* = *hure þu* (Gropp and Borgström). Skeat thought the initial letter a poorly formed *A* and supposed *Aretu* to be a contraction of *Ared þu*. He considered that the *J.* version supported this interpretation.

> [N]Eure þu bi þine lyue
> þe word of þine wyue

> to swiþe þu ne aréde.

After an examination, I have no doubt that this letter is a *V*.

425. MS., *iprarþed*. The first *r* is written above the line evidently as a correction, but the scribe forgot to delete the second *r*.
430. *J.*, *vordrye* for *T*'s *purchen*.
432. *J.*, "for to do þe gyle."
436. Evidently a reference to Eve's advice to eat the apple.

for hit is said *in* lede
cold red is quene red   440
hi ne saʒe it nocht bi-þan
þat god þing is god vimmo*n*
þe mon þad michte hire cnoþen
7 chesen hire from oþere.   444

uor it seiþ in þe led
cold red is cþene red.

(26)

Þus q*ua*d alfred
Be þu neuere to bold
to chiden aʒen oni scold
ne mid manie tales   448
to chiden aʒen alle dþales
Ne neuere þu biginne
to tellen neþe tidinges
at neuere nones mo*n*nis bord   452
ne haþe þu to fele þord
þe þise mon mid feþe þord
can fele biluken
7 sottis bold is sone iscote*n*   456
for-þi ich telle him for a dote
þad sait al is yþille
þanne he sulde ben stille
for ofte tunke brekit bo*n*   460
7 nauid hire selþe non.

ofte tunʒe breceþ bon.
þeih ne habbe him selue non.

---

439. *T.* and *Jms.* agree against *J.*, which
    offers the following reading:
      For hit seyþ in þe l[e]oþ
      as scumes forteoþ;
      hit is ifurn iseyd
      þat cold red is quene red;
      hu he is vnlede
      þat foleweþ hire rede.
    Such expansions are characteristic
    of the *J.* scribe. Note the three
    couplets thus obtained.
441. MS., *saþe. Hi,* for *I* or *ich,* shows
    T's use of the initial *h.*

442. *is* for *nis.*
443. MS., *cnospen.*
446–7. *J.* reads:
      Ne gabbe þu ne schotte
      ne chid þu wyþ none sotte.
448. *J.,* "manyes cunnes tales."
452. *J.,* "At nones fremannes borde."
454. *J.* has changed the word order in
    lines 454–55 in order to obtain a
    rime.
      Mid fewe word*e* wis mon
      fele biluken wel con.
456. *J., bolt.*

Maidstone

(27)

. . . .

Elde cummeþ to tune
mid fele unkuþe costes   464
7 dohþ þe man to elden
þat him self ne mai him þelden
it makeþ him þel un-muke
7 binimeþ him is mihte   468
if it so tideþ
þat tu her so longe abidest
7 tu in þin elde
þerldes þele þoldest   472
þi duȝeþe gin þu delen
þine dere frend
hþiles þine daȝes duȝe
7 tu þe selue laste muȝe   476
Haue þu none lefe
to þo þat after þe bilefe
to sune no to dohter
ne to none of þine foster   480
for feþe frend finde
þanne þe heþen funde
For he þat is uten biloken
he is inne for-ȝeten.   484

(28)

. . . .

if þu in þin elde

462. This section appears in Trinity, but
    is wanting in the Jesus MS. The
    Trinity version is practically identi-
    cal with Maidstone except for differ-
    ences of dialect and spelling.
    T., "þus quad alured."
465. *T., doþ.*
467. *T., vn-meke.*
472. *T., þeldest.*
476. *T., liue* for *laste.*

481. *T.* reads, "for feþe frend þe sculen
    finden."
484. *T.* inserts *sone* before *forȝeten.*
485. This section is given in Trinity and
    paraphrased by Spelman. It does
    not appear in the Jesus MS.
    T., "þus quad alured."
486–7. *T.* reads:
    ȝif þu i þin helde best
    þelþes bidelid.

best þele bi-delest
7 tu ne cunne þe leden   488
mid none kinne liste
ne þu miht mid strengþe
þe selue sternen
þanne þonke þu þi louerd   492
of alle hise lone
7 of þin oȝen lif
7 of þe daies liht
7 of alle þe murhþe   496
þat he þe for man makede
7 hƿider so þu þende
sai þu attenende
þurþe þat i-þurþe   500
þurþe godes ƿille.

Trinity

(29)

Þus qu*ad* alu*r*ed
þerldes þelþe
to þurmes scal þurþe*n*   504
7 alle cunne madmes

"If thou in thy old age art deprived
of wealth."
The active construction in *M*., in
which the verb *bi-delest* must be read
dividest with *þele* as an object and
best as an adverb, receives some
support from Spelman's paraphrase:
"If thou growest into Age, hast
Wealth. . . ." Cf. lines 473–74.
489. *T*. reads, *cunnes listis*.
491. *sternen*, error for *steren*. *T*.,
steren.
493. Spelman's paraphrase supports
M's *lone*: "then thank thy Lord
for all that he hath sent thee."
Borgström reads *loue* in *T*., but
Skeat is undecided between *loue*

and *lone*. In my opinion, *T*.
clearly reads *lone*. The evidence
of *M*. and *Sp*. leaves little doubt
that this is the proper reading.
504. Spelman's paraphrase confirms this
line: "worldly [printed *wordly*]
Wealth at last cometh to the
Worms. . . ."
J. reads:
    Alle world-ayhte
    schulle bi-cumen to nouhte.
A partial erasure in the manuscript
makes it uncertain whether the last
word on the line should be read
þurþen or *þurþien*. Borgström ac-
cepts *þurþen* in preference to
Skeat's reading *þurþien*.

to nocht sulen melten
7 ȝure lif
sal lutel lasten   508
for [þau] þu mon þeldest
al þis middellert
7 alle þe þelþe
þad þe[r]-inne þonit   512
Ne mist þu þi lif
lengen none þile
bote al þu it salt leten
one lutele stunde   516
7 al þi blisse
to bale sal i-þurþen
bote ȝif þu þurche
þille to *cri*ste   520
for biþeng þe þenne us selþen
to leden ure lif
so god us ginnid lere*n*

506. *J., to mixe.*
507. MS., *þure*, another example of the
     confusion of þ and ȝ.
     J. reads, "And vre owe lif."
509. *þau*, lacking in the MS. Its inser-
     tion is justified by the readings
     of Spelman and *J.*: Spelman, "And
     though one had the Rule"; *J.*, "For
     þeyh o mon wolde."
510. Spelman supports this line: "all
     this middle world." *J.*, "al þe
     worlde."
511–12. Confirmed by Spelman, "and
     of the Wealth in it." *J.*, *wunne.*
512. MS., *þe inne* for *þer-inne.*
513. *mist* for *miht.* The *T.* scribe fre-
     quently uses *st* for *ht.*
519. MS., *þif.*
521. MS., *þennis* with an erasure between
     e and *n*, which leads the reader to
     suppose he is dealing with two
     words. I have accepted Borg-
     ström's reading since his explana-
     tion is more logical than that of

Skeat. Borgström says (p. 63):
"*þennis* in the MS. is certainly
only a mistake for *þenne*. The
scribe had to write *þenne us*, but
seems to have run the two words
together, and noticing his mistake,
he added *us* without correcting his
error. Skeat reads (PA. ll. 400–
400*):
     For[þi] biþenk[e] we
     [on] þe wis us seluen.
In the foot-note he explains *þe uuis*
(for my reading *þennis*) as meaning
þe wis. But this is a daring explanation, since initial *uu* for *w* is
quite unknown in the MS. Besides,
Skeat's emendation does not give
a satisfactory meaning."
The reading *þenne* is supported by
J., "þanne vs selue."
523. Spelman's paraphrase supports *T.*
     in the use of *god* in this line: "as
     God hath taught us." *J.* reads
     Crist, perhaps because of the influ-

þenne muʒe þe þenen   524
þad he us þile þurþen
for sþo saide salomon
þe þise salomon
is þad þel doþ þis   528
hþile he in þis þerld is
euere at þen ende
he comid þer he hit findit.

(30)

Þus quad alured   532
sone min sþo leue
site me nu bisides
7 hich þe þile sigen
soþe þeþes.   536
Sone min ich fele
þad min her faleþidþ
7 min þlite is þan
7 min herte þoc   540
mine daʒis arren nei done
7 þe sulen unc to-delen
þenden ich me sal
to þis oþir þerlde   544
7 þu salt bileuen
in alle mine þelþe
sone min ich þe bidde
þu ard mi barin dere   548
þad þu þi folck be fader

ence of *Cristes* four lines above.

528–9. These lines have been altered in the manuscript. They originally read:

    þis is þad þel doþ
    hþile he is in þis þerld.   boþ.

In making the alteration, the scribe neglected to delete *boþ*.

J. reads:

    þe mon þat her wel deþ
    he cumeþ þar he lyen foþ.

530. MS., *þe nende, þe* occurring at the end of a line.

530–31. Spelman's paraphrase follows *T*. closely: "for at last he cometh where he findeth it."

J. reads:

    on his lyues ende
    he hit schal a-vynde.

532. Spelman's paraphrase corresponds closely to *T*'s reading of this paragraph.

7 for louerd
fader be þu ƿid child
7 be þu ƿideþis freⁿd   552
þe arme ginne þu froueren
7 þe ƿoke ginne þu coueren
þe ƿroⁿke ginne þu risten
mid alle þine misten   556
7 let þe sune mid laþe
7 loþien þe sulen driȝten
7 oþer alle oþir þinke
god be þe ful miⁿde   560
7 bide þad he þe rede
at alle þine dedis
þe bet [he] sal þe filsten
to doⁿ al þine ƿille.   564

(31)

Þus qᵤₐd aluᵣₑd
Sone miⁿ so dere
do so ich þe lere
be þu ƿis on þi ƿord   568
7 ƿar o þine speche
þenne sulen þe loþien
leden alle
þe ȝunge mon do þu laþe   572
þad helde lat is lond haþen
Drunken mon ȝif þu mestes
iⁿ ƿeis oþer iⁿ stretes
þu ȝef him þe ƿeie reme   576
7 let him ford gliden
þanne mist þu þi lond

555–6. Following his usual practice of
writing *st* for *ht*, the Trinity scribe
writes *risten* and *misten*.

558. *sulen*, probably an error for *sal*.
Spelman's paraphrase gives the
singular.

562. Spelman's reading, "in all thy
need," indicates that the Cotton

MS. read *nede*, which also preserves
the rime.

563. *he*, wanting in the MS. Spelman
supports the insertion.

565. The remaining lines of the *Proverbs*
are found only in *T.*, with the exception of lines 611–12 in James.

574. *mestes* for *metes*. MS., *þif*.

mit frendchipe helden.
Sone þu best bus þe sot   580
of bismare þord
7 bet hin siþen þer-mide
þad him ginne to smerten
7 baren ich þe bidde   584
ʒif þu on benche sitthest
7 þu þen beuir hore sixst
þe biforen stonden
buch þe from þi sete   588
7 bide him sone þer-to
þanne þelle he saʒin
sone one his þorde
þel þorþe þe þid   592
þad þe first taite
sete þanne seiþin
bisiden him seluen
for of him þu mist leren   596
listis 7 fele þeues
þe baldure þu mist ben
for lere þu his reides
for þe helder mon me mai of- 600
    riden
betere þenne of-reden.

(32)

þus quad alured
Sone min so dere

580. Skeat gives *bus* as the contracted form of *buʒes*, *pr. 2 s.*, "thou shalt bow." He supplies *to* and translates (p. 68), "Son, thou wilt best advance towards the foolish man of abusive speech." See p. 68 for his reasons. This interpretation is at variance with the idea in ll. 445–49.

Borgström (pp. 65–66) interprets *bus* to mean *bow, bend from, avoid.* Advice to avoid a fool in anger, but later to beat him with his own words (*þer-mide*), i.e., reproach him with his words, until he begins to smart, is somewhat more consistent with the earlier passage (lines 445–9) on behavior toward fools.

Another possibility is the translation of *bus* as *shalt bend* or *turn:* "Son, thou shalt best turn the foolish man from abusive speech."

585. MS., *þif.*   590. MS., *saþin.*

ches þu neuere to fere   604
þen luþere lusninde mon
for he þe ꝑile ꝑrake don
from þe ꝑode þu mitht te
    faren
ꝑid ꝑilis 7 ꝑid armes   608
ac þanne þu hid lest ꝑenest
þe luþere þe bisꝑiket
þe bicche bitit ille   þe biche biteþ ille.
þau he berke stille   612   þoh he berce stille
so deit þe lusninde luþere mon   . . . . Explicit liber Alfredi
ofte þen he darit don   MS. Th. Allen.
þau he be ꝑiþ-uten stille
he bit ꝑiþ-innin hille   616
7 al he bi-fulit his frend
þen he him vnfoldit.

(33)

Þus qꝓad aluꝛed
leꝑe sone dere   620
ne ches þu neuere to fere
þen hokerfule lese mon
for he þe ꝑole gile don
he ꝑole stelin þin haite   624
    7 keren
7 listeliche onsuerren
so longe he uole be bi
he uole brinhin on 7 tuenti
to nout for soþe ich tellit þe 628

607. MS., fron.
614. Perhaps ꝑen. The T. scribe is
    careless in making a clear distinc-
    tion between þ and ꝑ. Skeat reads
    ꝑen, but Borgström, þen, other
    examples of which occur in the
    MS. See 618, etc.
624. See Skeat (p. 69) for a discussion of

keren. He believes that keren is the
M.E. cüren, to choose, a verb
formed from O.E. cyre, choice. He
translates: "he will steal thy goods
and choose (from them)."
Compare L.O.E. *cyrne (cf. Norw.
kyrne). See N.E.D., kern, sb².

7 oþer he þole liȝen 7 hokerful
  ben
þuru hoker 7 lesing þe aloþed
alle men þat hen ycnoþed
ac nim to þe a stable mon   632
þat þord 7 dede bisette con
7 multeplien heure god
a sug fere þe his help in
  mod.

      (34)

Þus quad alured   636
leue sone dere
ne ches þu neuere to fere
littele mon ne long ne red
ȝif þu þld don after mi red.   640

      (35)

Þe luttele mon he his so rei
ne mai non him þonin nei
so þord he þole him seluen ten
þat is louird maister he þolde 644
  ben
bute he mote him seluen
  þruden
he þole maken fule luden
he þole grennen cocken 7
  chiden
7 heþere faren mid vn-luden 648
ȝif þu me þld ileuen
ne mai me neuer him quemen.

629. MS., *liþen.* Gropp suggested the emendation.
632. MS., *þe to þe.*
634. *heure.* Borgström believes this is not *eure* (your) since *T.* uses *ȝure* in all other instances. He thinks that it stands for *always;* compare *heþere,* line 648.
635. MS., *moð.*
638. MS., *neuerre.*
640. MS., *þif.*
643. *þord* for *þorð.*
649. MS., *þif.*

(36)

Þe lonke mon is leþe-bei
selde comid is herte rei   652
he hauit stoni herte
no þing him ne smerteþ
bi ford daȝes he is aferd
of sticke 7 ston in huge þerd   656
ȝif he fallit in þe fen
he þeþ[t]it ut after men
ȝif he slit in-to a dige
he is ded þiterliche.   660

(37)

Þe rede mon he is a quet
for he þole þe þin iþil red
he is cocker þef 7 horeling
scolde of þreche-dome he is   664
    king.
Hic ne sige nout bi-þan
þat moni ne ben gentile man
þuru þis lore 7 genteleri
he amendit huge companie.   668

---

652. Borgström believes *rei* is a scribal error for *nei*, a conjecture which he thinks borne out by the sense of the two following lines. It seems to me that *rei* (for *reih*, O.E. *hrēoh*) meaning *fierce*, is very appropriate. I translate these lines thus: "Seldom does his heart become fierce or passionate. He has a stony heart. Nothing makes him smart."

655. *ford*. *Forð-dæges* means "at close of day." Gropp points out for comparison Mark VI, 35, of the translation made by Wyclif and his followers: "Whanne it was forth daies,"—when it was late in the day. See *forth*, 4b, *N.E.D.*

657. MS., *þif*.

658. *þeþit*. Borgström believes this an error for *þeptit* or *þeutit*, (O.E. *þeotan, yell* or *howl*).

659. MS., *þif, adige*.

661. *a quet* for *a qued*.

667. *þis*, perhaps an error for *þis*.

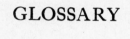

GLOSSARY

GLOSSARY

[Effort has been made to give the Old English forms from which the words of the poem derive, in order that the resemblance to the language of the early period and the almost complete freedom from foreign influence may emphasize the early date of the *Proverbs*.

Words beginning with ʒ will be found after *g;* those beginning with þ or ð after *t*. No distinction has been made between words beginning with *w* and with *p*. For convenience and consistency, *w*, or *g*, has been used instead of *p* or ʒ in the spelling of the Old English source-words.

The usual abbreviations for parts of speech have been employed. If the person of a verb is not otherwise indicated, the third person is to be understood.]

a, *indef. art.;* a, *T*.635, 659. (O.E. *ān*.)

abidest, *pr. 2 s.;* abidest, *M*.470. (O.E. *ābīdan*.)

ac, *conj.;* but, *M*.127, 143, 250; *T*.354, etc. (O.E. *ac*.)

aferd, *pp.;* afraid, frightened, *T*.655. (O.E. *āfæran, pp. āfæred*.)

aʒen, *prep.;* against, *T*.447, 449; *awen, M*.124; *aʒenes, M*.126. (O.E. *ongēan*.)

ahte, *sb.;* property, *M*.142; *athte, T*.267, 270. (O.E. *æht*.)

ahte, *pt. subj. s.;* were to possess, *Jms*.98. (O.E. *āgan, pt. subj. s. āhte*.)

akeres, *sb.;* acres, *M*.99; *aceres, Jms*.99. (O.E. *æcer*.)

al, *adv.;* altogether, *M*.141; *T*.617. (O.E. *eall*.)

al, all, alle, ale, *adj.* or *pro.;* all; *alre, gen. pl.,* of all, *Sp*.92; *Jms*.92; *M*.158. (O.E. *eall, gen. pl. eallra*.)

ale, *sb.;* ale (?), *M*.249. (O.E. *ealu*.)

Alfred, Alfrede, *pr. n.;* Alfred, *W*.9, 17; *Jms*.9, 17, etc.; *Alured, W*.25; *Jms*.25, etc.; *Aluerd, Sp*.61, 71, etc.; *alureid, T*.346. (O.E. *Ælfrēd*.)

Alfrich, *pr. n.;* Ælfric, *W*.7; *Jms*.7. (O.E. *Ælfric*.)

aloþed, *pr. pl. as fut.;* will loathe, *T*.630. (O.E. *laðian* with intensifying prefix.)

al so, *just as, T*.379.

amendit, *pr. s.;* amends, improves, *T*.668. (O.F. *amender*.)

among, *prep.;* among; *þer among,* thereamong, *M*.251. (O.E. *ongemang, amang*.)

an, *conj.;* and, *M*.100, etc. (O.E. *and, ond*.)

an, *pr. s.;* wishes, *M*.216.   (O.E. *unnan, pr. s. an(n)*.)

appel, *sb.;* apple, *M*.334; *Jms.* 334.   (O.E. *æppel*.)

ard, *pr. 2 s.;* art, *T*.548.

areȝe, *adj.* as *sb.;* cowardly or evil-hearted man, *M*.204, 212, 220, 221.
   (O.E. *earg, earh*.)

arme, *adj. pl.* or *sb.;* poor, *Sp*.39; *T*.553.   (O.E. *earm, pl. earme*.)

armes, *sb.;* arms, weapons, *T*.608.   (Lat. *arma*.)

armþe, *sb.;* poverty, *T*.411.   (O.E. *earmþu*.)

arren, *pr. pl.;* are, *T*.541.

at, *prep.;* at, *W*.1; *Jms*.1, etc.; *ate, T*.394; an error for *al* (all), *M*.116.
   (O.E. *æt*.)

at-go, *pr. subj. s.;* may depart from, *M*.196.   (O.E. *āgān*.)

athte, see *ahte*.

attende, *adv.;* behind his back, *M*.322.   (O.E. *æt-hindan*.)

attenende, *adv. expression;* at the end, *M*.499.   (O.E. *æt þe ende*.)

aþeling, *sb.;* nobleman, prince, *M*.72; *Jms*.72.   (O.E. *æþeling*.)

awei, *adv.;* away, *T*.377.   (O.E. *aweg*.)

awen, see *aȝen*.

baldure, *comp. adj.;* bolder, *T*.598.   (O.E. *bealdra, baldra*.)

bale, *sb.;* evil, grief, bale, *T*.518.   (O.E. *bealo, bealu*.)

bale-siþes, *sb.;* misfortunes, paths leading to destruction, *M*.292.   (O.E.
   bealu-siþ.)

banne, *vb. inf.;* curse, *M*.237.   (O.E. *bannan*.)

baren, *sb.;* child, bairn, *T*.584; *barin, T*.548.   See *bern*.   (O.E. *bearn*.)

bed, *pr. s.;* is, *T*.425.   (O.E. *biþ*.)

beme, *dat. s.;* tree, bough, *M*.335; *Jms*.335.   (O.E. *beam*.)

ben, *vb. inf.;* be, *Jms*.64, 360; *Sp*.64; *M*.261; *T*.355, 360, etc.; *pr. pl.*,
   are, *M*.73; *Jms*.73; *T*.666 (*pl.* for *s.*).   (O.E. *bēon, pr. pl. bēoþ*.)

benche, *dat. s.;* bench, seat, *T*.585.   (O.E. *benc, dat. s. bence*.)

berke, *pr. subj. s.;* bark, *T*.612; *berce, Jms*.612.   (O.E. *beorcan*.)

bern, *sb.;* child, bairn, *M*.226, 231, 239, etc.   See *baren*.   (O.E. *bearn*.)

bes, *pr. 2 s. as fut.;* shalt be, *T*.378.   (O.E. *bist*.)

best, *adv.;* best, in the best way, *T*.580; *M*.487.   (O.E. *betst*.)

bet, *pr. s. as fut.;* shall be, *T*.402.   (O.E. *biþ*.)

bet, *imp. s.;* beat, *T*.582.   (O.E. *bēatan*.)

betere, *comp. adj.;* better, *M*.185, 241, 243; *adv., M*.310; *T*.382, 601.
   (O.E. *betera*.)

beth, *comp. adj.;* better, *M*.232.   See *bett*.   (O.E. *bet, bett*.)

bett, *adv.;* better, *T*.372; *bet, T*.563.   (O.E. *bett, bet*.)

beuir, *adj. s.;* feeble, trembling, *T*.586. (Cf. M.E. *beveren,* to tremble. Cf. O.E. *bifian,* to tremble. See *bevar, N.E.D.*)

beþen, *vb. inf.;* bend, *T*.354. (O.E. *bēgan.*)

bi, *prep.;* by, *T*.266, 626 (*þe* omitted); *bir, Jms*.266. (O.E. *be, bī.*)

bicche, *sb.;* bitch, *T*.611; *biche, Jms*.611. (O.E. *bicce.*)

bicome, *pt. subj. s.;* would befit, *M*.185, 310; *T*.382. (O.E. *becuman.*)

bidde, *pr. 1 s.;* ask, pray, *T*.547, 584; *bide, imp. s., T*.561, 589 (invite). (O.E. *biddan, imp. s. bide.*)

bi-delest, *pr. 2 s.;* dividest, *M*.487. (O.E. *bedǽlan.*)

bi-foren, *prep.;* before, *M*.285; *T*.587; *adv.,* before thy or his face, *M*.213, *T*.371; *bi-fore, M*.321. (O.E. *beforan.*)

bi-fulit, *pr. s.;* befouls, brings shame on, *T*.617. (O.E. *befȳlan.*)

bigan, *pt. s.;* began, *T*.436; *biginne, imp. s.,* begin, *T*.450. (O.E. *beginnan, pt. s. begann.*)

biȝete, *dat. s.;* share of thy gains, *T*.367. (O.E. *begēat.*)

bi-ȝete, *pr. subj. 2 s.;* mayst obtain, *T*.366. (O.E. *begietan.*)

bi-hath, *pr. s.;* promises, *M*.320. (O.E. *behātan.*)

bihinden, *adv.;* behind, *M*.214; *T*.371. (O.E. *behindan.*)

bihoueþ, *pr. s.;* behoveth, *Jms*.83; *behoveth, Sp*.83. (O.E. *behōfian.*)

bileuen, *vb. inf.;* survive, remain, *T*.545; *bilefe, pr. pl., M*.478. (O.E. *belǽfan.*)

bilif, *sb.;* sustenance, *Jms*.92; *Sp*.92. (O.E. *bīleofa.*)

biluken, *vb. inf.;* comprehend, shut in, lock, *T*.455; *biloken, pp.,* locked, *M*.483. (O.E. *belūcan, pp. belocen.*)

bi-menen, *vb. inf.;* lament, *M*.151; *bimeneþ, pr. s.* as *fut.,* will condole with, *M*.213. (O.E. *bemǽnan.*)

binimeþ, *pr. s.;* deprives of, *M*.468. (O.E. *beniman.*)

binnen, *prep.;* within, *T*.416; *binne, Jms*.416. (O.E. *binnan.*)

bir, see *bi.*

biscopes, *sb.;* bishops, *W*.3; *Jms*.3. (O.E. *bisceop, biscop.*)

bisette, *vb. inf.;* use well, *T*.633. (O.E. *besettan.*)

bisiden, *prep.;* beside, *T*.595; *bisides, T*.534. (O.E. *be* (*prep.* by), *sīdan* (*dat. s.* of side).)

bismare þord, abusive speech, *T*.581. (O.E. *bismer,* insult.)

bi-spiken, *vb. inf.;* betray, *M*.332 (with *scal* understood from the previous line); *bispiket, pr. s.* as *fut., T*.610. (O.E. *beswīcan.*)

bit, biteþ, *pr. s.;* bites, *T*.616; *Jms*.611; *bitit, T*.611. (O.E. *bītan.*)

biteleþ, *pr. s.* as *fut.;* will blame, *M*.214. (O.E. *tǽlan* with prefix *be.*)

biter, *adj. s.;* bitter, *M*.336; *bitter, Jms*.336. (O.E. *biter.*)

bitideþ, *pr. s.;* happens, *M*.225, 306. (O.E. *tīdan* with prefix *be.*)

bitoȝen, *pp.;* bestowed, employed, *M*.136. (O.E. *betēon, pp. betogen.*)

bi-tƿenen, *prep.;* between, among, *M*.305. (O.E. *betwēonum.*)

bi-þan, *adv.;* thereby, *T*.441, 665. (O.E. *be þam.*)

biþeng, *pr. subj. 1 pl.;* let us bethink ourselves, *T*.521. (O.E. *biþencan.*)

biþilen, *vb. inf.;* beguile, *T*.432. (O.E. *wīglian* with prefix *be.*)

blessedness, *sb.;* blessedness, *Sp*.50. (Cf. O.E. *bletsian*, to bless, *bletsung*, blessing.)

blisse, *sb.;* bliss, joy, *Sp*.49; *M*.224; *T*.517. (O.E. *bliss.*)

bliþe, *adv.;* happily, *T*.417; *Jms*.417. (O.E. *bliðe.*)

blod, *sb.;* blood; *leche blod*, body blood, *M*.259. (O.E. *blōd.*)

boc-lered, *adj.* or *sb.;* book-learned (men), *W*.4; *Jms*.4, 65; *Sp*.65. (O.E. *bōc*, book; *pp. lǣred*, taught.)

bode, *sb.;* command, *M*.240. (O.E. *bod.*)

boge, see *sadel boȝe.*

bold, *sb.;* bolt, arrow, *T*.456. (O.E. *bolt.*)

bold, *adj. s.;* bold, *T*.446. (O.E. *beald, bald.*)

bon, *sb.;* bone, *Jms*.460; *T*.460. (O.E. *bān.*)

bord, *sb.;* board, table, *T*.452. (O.E. *bord.*)

boren, *pp.;* born, *M*.186. (O.E. *beran. pp. boren* or *geboren.*)

bote, *conj.;* but, *T*.515; *bote ȝif*, unless, *T*.519. (O.E. *bute.*)

boþen, *pro.;* both, *T*.381. (O.E. *bēgen (bā, bū, bō).*)

breceþ, *pr. s.;* breaks, *Jms*.460, *brekit*, *T*.460. (O.E. *brecan.*)

briht, *adj. s.;* bright, fair, *M*.335; *brihte*, *Jms*.335. (O.E. *beorht.*)

bringen, *vb. inf.;* bring, *T*.268; *Jms*.268; *brinhin*, *T*.627; *brinȝeþ*, *pr. s.*, *Jms*.275; *M*.275; *T*.438; *brinhit*, *T*.275. (O.E. *bringan.*)

brinhin, brinhit, see *bringen.*

buch, for *būh, imp. s.;* bow, *T*.588. (O.E. *būgan.*)

bure, *dat. s.;* bower, lady's room, *M*.338; *Jms*.338. (O.E. *būr.*)

bury, *dat. s.;* dwelling, *T*.268; *burie, T*.416; *buri, Jms*.268, 416. (O.E. *burg, burh; dat. s. byrig.*)

bus, see note, line 580.

bute, *conj.;* unless, *T*.645. (O.E. *būton, būtan.*)

can, *pr. s.;* knows, can, *M*.208; *T*.434, 455; *con, T*.633. (O.E. *cunnan, pr. s. can.*)

catt, *sb.;* cat, kitten, *T*.356. (O.E. *cat, catt.*)

ceneliche, *adv.;* keenly, *Jms*.84; *Sp*.84. (O.E. *cēnlīce.*)

chariweth, *pr. s.;* returns, *M*.81. (O.E. *cierran, cerran.*)

cherl, *sb.;* peasant, *Jms*.88; *Sp*.88. (O.E. *ceorl.*)

chesen, *vb. inf.;* choose, *Jms*.266; *T*.266, 444; *chesed, pr. s.*, *T*.273; *ches, imp. s.*, *T*.604, 621, 638. (O.E. *cēosan.*)

chiden, *vb. inf.;* chide, quarrel, *T.*447, 449, 647. (O.E. *cīdan.*)

child, *sb.;* child, *M.*224; *T.*551. (O.E. *cild.*)

churche, *sb.;* church, *Jms.*87; *chureche, Sp.*87. (O.E. *cyrice, cirice, cyrce, circe.*)

cing, *sb.;* king, *Sp.*63; *cinʒ, Jms.*63. (O.E. *cyning, cyng.*)

clerc, *sb.;* clerk, learned man, *W.*19; *Jms.*19, 76; *M.*76. (O.E. *clerc.*)

cniht, *sb.;* knight, *Jms.*76, 83; *Sp.*83; *M.*76; *cnihtes, pl., W.*6; *Jms.*6. (O.E. *cniht.*)

cnoþen, *vb. inf.;* know, *Jms.*84; *T.*443. (O.E. *cnāwan.*)

cocken, *vb. inf.;* strut, fight, behave like a cock, *T.*647. (Verb formed from O.E. *coc,* cock. See *cock* v.(1), *N.E.D.*)

cocker, *sb.;* fighter, *T.*663. (O.E. *coc* (*cocc*) plus *er.*)

cold, *adj. s.;* evil, *Jms.*440; *T.*440. (O.E. *ceald, cald.*)

comid, *pr. s.* as *fut.;* will come, *T.*531, 652 (becomes). (O.E. *cuman.*)

companie, *sb.;* company, *T.*668. (O.F. *compaignie.*)

con, see *can.*

costes, *sb.;* habits, traits, ways, *T.*269; *M.*464. (O.E. *cost,* condition or mode.) (O.E. *cyst,* virtue.)

cotlif, *sb.;* life in a cottage, *Jms.*275; *M.*275; *T.*275. (O.E. *cot-līf.*)

coueren, *vb. inf.;* protect, *T.*554. (O.F. *cuvrir.*)

Crist, Christ, *Sp.*42; *M.*117; gen., *Sp.*64; *criste,* gen., *Jms.*64; *Criste,* dat., *Jms.*34; *Sp.*34; *T.*520; acc., *Jms.*42. (O.E. *Crīst.*)

cumeþ, *pr. s.;* comes, *M.*235; *cummeþ, M.*463. (O.E. *cuman.*)

cunne, gen. *pl.;* of (all) kinds, *T.*505. (O.E. *cynn,* gen. *pl. cynna.*)

cunne, *pr. subj. 2 s.;* should be able, *M.*488; *pr. subj. s.,* know, *Jms.*67; *Sp.*67; *cuþe, pt. subj. 2 s.,* shouldst know, *J.*269. (O.E. *cunnan.*)

cuþe, see *cunne.*

cuþen, *vb. inf.;* make known, tell, *M.*331. (O.E. *cȳðan.*)

cpaþ, *pt. s.;* quoth, *W.*25; *Jms.*25; *cwath, Sp.*61, etc. (O.E. *cpeðen, pt. s. cpæþ.*)

cpene, gen. *s.;* woman's, *Jms.*440. (O.E. *cwēn,* gen. *cwēne.*)

cwethen, *sb.;* sayings, *Sp.*35. (O.E. *cwide.*)

daʒes, *sb.;* days, *M.*475; *daʒis, T.*541; *daies,* gen. *s., M.*495. (O.E. *dæg,* gen. *s. dæges, nom. & acc. pl. dagas.*)

darit, for *dear it, pr. s.;* dares, *T.*614. (O.E. *durran, pr. s. dear.*)

ded, *adj. s.;* dead, *T.*660. (O.E. *dēad.*)

dede, *sb.;* deed, *T.*633; *dedes, pl., T.*426; *dedis, T.*562; *deden, dat. pl., M.*75; *Jms.*75. (O.E. *dæd, dat. pl. dædum.*)

deʒh, *pr. s.;* avails, *T.*375. (O.E. *dugan, pr. s. dēah.*)

deit, for *deþ, pr. s.;* does, *T*.613. See *don.* (O.E. *dōn.*)

delen, *vb. inf.;* distribute, share, *M*.473. (O.E. *dǣlan.*)

demen, *pr. pl.;* judge, *M*.77; *Jms*.77. (O.E. *dēman.*)

dere, *adj. s. & pl.;* dear, *Sp*.38; *M*.474; *T*.189, 548, etc. (O.E. *dēore.*)

derlinȝ, *sb.;* darling, *W*.11; *Jms*.11. (O.E. *dēorling.*)

desiȝeþ, see *disiȝeþ.*

dige, *dat. s.;* ditch, *T*.659. (O.E. *dīc.*)

disiȝeþ, *pr. s.;* acts foolishly, *M*.251; *desiȝeþ*, *M*.253, probably an error for *desiende, T*.253 (acting foolishly). (O.E. *dysian.*)

do, *imp. s.;* do, *T*.567; with *lape*, administer law to, *T*.572. See *don.* (O.E. *dōn, imp. s. dō.*)

dohter, *dat. s.;* daughter, *M*.479. (O.E. *dohtor.*)

dom, *sb.;* judgment, *M*.80; *domes, gen. s., M*.170. (O.E. *dōm, gen. s. dōmes.*)

don, *vb. inf.;* do, *T*.351, 435, 564, etc.; *doþ, pr. s., Jms*.103; *M*.103, 257, 259; *T*.528; *dohþ, M*.465 (makes); *done, pp., T*.541. (O.E. *dōn, pr. s. dēþ.*)

dote, *sb.;* fool, *T*.457. (O.F. *(re)doter* (?).) See *dote* v.(1), *N.E.D.*

doþ, see *don.*

dreden, *pr. subj. 2 pl.;* may dread or be in awe of, *Jms*.41; *drede, Sp*.41. (O.E. *drǣdan.*)

dreiȝe, *sb.;* annoyance, *T*.362. (Cf. O.E. *drēogan,* to endure.) Skeat thinks *dreiȝe* may originally have been *treȝe,* affliction, a word very often found in company with *tene,* which occurs in the next line.

dreri, *adj. s.;* sad, *T*.279. (O.E. *drēorig.*)

Drihten, the Lord, *Jms*.42, 405; *Sp*.42; *M*.180; *drichen, T*.405; *Drichtin, M*.169; *driȝten, T*.558. (O.E. *dryhten.*)

drinken, *vb. inf.;* drink, *M*.248; *drinkeþ, pr. s., M*.250; *drunken, pp., M*.246; *T*.574. (O.E. *drincan, pp. druncen.*)

driven, *vb. inf.;* drive, *Sp*.91; *driuen, Jms*.91; *pp.,* (be) driven, *M*.179; *driuist, pr. 2 s., T*.377. (O.E. *drīfan.*)

duȝe, *pr. pl.;* last, *M*.475. (O.E. *dugan, pr. pl. dugon.*)

duȝeðe, *sb.;* wealth, *Jms*.404; *duȝeþe, M*.473; *duȝe, T*.404. (O.E. *duguð.*)

dure, *dat. s.;* door, *M*.81. (O.E. *duru.*)

dusi, *adj. s.;* foolish, *M*.299. (O.E. *dysig.*)

duste, *dat. s.;* dust, *M*.179. (O.E. *dūst.*)

dȝales, *sb.;* fools, *T*.449. (O.E. *gedwola,* error, one who errs.)

ec, *adv.;* also, *W*.9; *Jms*.9, 33; *Sp*.33. (O.E. *ēac.*)

edi[e], *adj. pl.;* rich, *Sp*.39. (O.E. *ēadig.*)

ednesse, *sb.;* prosperity, *M*.132. (O.E. *eādnes.*)

efre, *adv.;* ever, *M*.163, 180, 247, etc. (O.E. *æfre.*)

efrilches, *adj. s.;* each, *M*.80. (O.E. *æghwilc.*)

eft, *adv.;* again, *M*.315. (O.E. *eft.*)

egleche, *adj. pl.;* bold, valiant, *W*.6; *Jms*.6. (O.E. *aglæca,* fierce warrior, (Skeat, p. 53).)

ehte, *sb.;* property, *Jms*.267, 410. See *ahte.* (O.E. *æht.*)

elde, *sb.;* old age, *M*.131, 235, 463, etc. (O.E. *ieldu, yldu.*)

elden, *vb. inf.;* grow old, *M*.465. (O.E. *ieldan, yldian.*)

eldere, *gen. pl.;* of elders or parents, *M*.142. (O.E. *ieldra, yldra.*)

ende, *sb.;* end, *M*.167; *T*.530. (O.E. *ende.*)

En3le, *gen. pl.;* Englishmen's, *W*.10, 11, 26; *Jms*.10, 11, 26; *Sp*.62, 71*. (O.E. *Engla.*)

En3elond, *pr. n.;* England, *W*.17, 24; *Jms*.24; *on3elond, Jms*.17; *En3lond, Jms*.12; *En3elonde, W*.12. (O.E. *Engla-land.*)

eni, *adj. s.;* any, *T*.428. (O.E. *ænig.*)

er, *adv.;* previously, ere, *M*.309. (O.E. *ær.*)

eren, *sb.;* ears, *M*.314. (O.E. *ēare, pl. ēaran.*)

erl, *sb.;* earl, *W*.7; *Jms*.72; *M*.72; *erle, Jms*.7; *erles, pl., W*.5; *Jms*.5. (O.E. *eorl.*)

erre, *sb.;* ire, *M*.182. (O.E. *yrre, ierre.*)

erþe, *sb.;* earth, *Jms*.103; *M*.103. (O.E. *eorþe.*)

euen, *sb.;* evening, *M*.262. (O.E. *æfen.*)

euenliche, *adv.;* impartially, *Jms*.77; *M*.77. (O.E. *efenlīce.*)

euere, *adv.;* ever, *T*.530; *euuere, T*.420. (O.E. *æfre.*)

fader, *sb.;* father, *T*.549, 551; *gen. s., Jms*.338; *M*.224, 338. (O.E. *fæder, gen. s. fæder.*)

faire, *adj. as sb.;* fair woman, *T*.272; *faires,* fine things, *Jms*.408; *T*.408. (O.E. *fæger.*)

faire, *adv.;* fairly, *M*.320, 321. (O.E. *fægere, fægre.*)

falepidþ, *pr. s.;* changes color, *T*.538. (O.E. *fealwian.*)

fallit, *pr. s.;* falls, *T*.657. (O.E. *feallan.*)

faren, *vb. inf.;* go, travel, *T*.401; go about, *T*.648; *te faren,* escape, *T*.607; *fare, pr. subj. s.,* may fare, *Jms*.94; *Sp*.94; *farrest*[*u*], *pr. 2 s.* as *fut., T*.396. (O.E. *faran.*)

faste, *adv.;* fast, *Jms*.409; *T*.409. (O.E. *fæste.*)

fe, *sb.;* property, *M*.149; *T*.380. (O.E. *feoh.*)

fei3e, *adj. s.;* fated to die, *M*.163. (O.E. *fæge.*)

felde, *dat. s.;* field, *M*.162. (O.E. *feld, dat. s. felde.*)

fele, *adj. pl.;* many, *W.*3, 4; *Jms.*3, 4; *T.*453, 464, 597; as *substantive,* much, *T.*455. (O.E. *fela.*)

fele, *pr. 1 s.;* feel, *T.*537. (O.E. *fēlian.*)

fen, *sb.;* mud, *T.*657. (O.E. *fen(n).*)

fend, *sb.;* enemy, *M.*308. (O.E. *fēond.*)

fere, *sb.;* companion, *M.*199; *T.*604, 621, 635, 638. (O.E. *(ge)fēra.*)

fere, for *ferh, sb.;* life, *M.*164. (O.E. *feorh.*)

feþe, *adj. pl.;* few, *M.*481; *T.*454. (O.E. *fēawe.*)

fikel, *adj. s.;* fickle, deceitful, *M.*329. (O.E. *ficol.*)

filsten, *vb. inf.;* help, assist, *T.*563. (O.E. *fylstan.*)

findit, *pr. s.* as *fut.;* will find, *T.*531; *finde, pr. 1 pl.* as *fut.*, *M.*481. (O.E. *findan.*)

first, *adv.;* first, *T.*593. (O.E. *fyrst.*)

flesce, *dat. s.;* flesh, meat, *M.*257. (O.E. *flǣsc.*)

fokel, *adj. s.* as *sb.;* false woman, *T.*273; *adv.*, deceitfully, *M.*322. (Corruption from O.E. *ficol* (?).)

foken, *pr. pl.;* act deceitfully, *M.*305. (O.E. *fācen,* deceit; *fǣcne,* deceitful.)

folce, *dat. s.*, for *gen. folces;* of the people, *Sp.*53; *folck[e], dat. s.*, *T.*549. (O.E. *folc.*)

foleþid, *pr. s.;* follows, *T.*437. (O.E. *folgian.*)

fon, *sb.;* foes, *M.*148, 286. (O.E. *gefā, pl. gefān.*)

for-cuþ, *adj. s.;* hostile, *M.*330. (O.E. *forcūþ.*)

ford, *adv.;* forth, *T.*577; *ford daȝes,* see note to line 655. (O.E. *forð.*)

for drunken, *pp.;* very drunk, *M.*252. (O.E. *fordrincan, pp. fordruncen.*)

for-fare, *vb. inf.;* suffer, *M.*198. (O.E. *forfaran.*)

for-ȝeten, *pp.;* forgotten, *M.*484. (O.E. *forgietan, forgytan.*)

for-helet, *imp.* combined with *pro. it;* conceal it, *M.*220. (O.E. *forhelan.*)

for-hidet, *imp.* combined with *pro. it;* hide it, *M.*219. (O.E. *forhȳdan.*)

for-leseþ, *pr. s.;* loses, *M.*184. (O.E. *forlēosan.*)

forloren, *pp.;* lost entirely, *T.*380. (O.E. *forlēosan, pp. forloren.*)

for sþuken, for *for-swunken, pp.;* tired out with work, *T.*352. (O.E. *swincan,* to work, with intensifying prefix.)

forþ, *adv.;* forth, *M.*147. (O.E. *forð.*)

for-þi, *adv.;* therefore, *M.*140; *T.*457. (O.E. *for-þȳ.*)

foster, *sb.;* offspring, *M.*480. (O.E. *fōster.*)

fre, *adj. s.;* liberal, freely bestowed, *T.*367. (O.E. *frēo.*)

fremde, *adj.* as *sb.;* a stranger, *M.*106; *fremðe, Jms.*106. (O.E. *fremde, fremðe.*)

frend, *sb.;* friend, *M.*107, 309, etc.; *T.*366, 376, etc.; *pl.*, *Sp.*38; *M.*474, 481; *frende, acc. s.*, *Jms.*107. (O.E. *frēond, pl. frēond.*)

frendchipe, *sb.;* friendship, *T*.395, 579.   (O.E. *frēondscipe*.)

friþ, *sb.;* peace, *Jms*.88; *Sp*.88.   (O.E. *friþ*.)

fro, *prep.;* from, *M*.197.   See *þer-fro.*   (O.E. *fram, fra*.)

frofre, *sb.;* comfort, *W*.26; *Jms*.26; *Sp*.54, 62, 71*.   (O.E. *frōfor*.)

frond, *sb.;* friend, *M*.300.   See *frend.*   (O.E. *frēond*.)

froueren, *vb. inf.;* comfort, *T*.553.   (O.E. *frōferian, frōfrian*.)

ful, *adj. s.;* full, *M*.340; *full, Jms*.340; *ful, adv.,* very, well, *M*.216; *T*.560.
   (O.E. *ful, full*.)

fule, *adj. pl.;* foul, shameful, *T*.646.   (O.E. *fūl*.)

funde, *pr. 1 pl.;* go, depart, *M*.482.   (O.E. *fundian*.)

furst, *adv.;* first, *M*.238.   See *first.*   (O.E. *fyrst*.)

gadelig, *sb.;* companion, low fellow, *M*.342.   (O.E. *gædeling*.)

genteleri, *sb.;* gentlemanly conduct, *T*.667.   (O.F.*gentil(adj.*) with suffix
   to form noun.)

gentile, *adj. s.;* gentle, *T*.666.   (O.F. *gentil*.)

gile, *sb.;* guile, *T*.623.   (O.F. *guile*.)

gin, ginne, *imp. s.;* begin, do, *M*.140, 325, 473; *T*.553–5; *ʒin, Jms*.265,
   406; *ginnid, pr. s.,* doth, *T*.523.   (O.E. *onginnan* or *beginnan*.)

ginne, *pr. subj. s.;* it may begin, *T*.583.   (O.E. *beginnan*.)

gleu, *adj. s.;* wise, prudent, *T*.386.   (O.E. *glēaw*.)

gliden, *vb. inf.;* glide, *T*.577.   (O.E. *glīdan*.)

glod, see *gold.*

god, God, *Sp*.45; *T*.523, 560; *godes, gen., W*.20; *M*.134, 143, 182, etc.;
   ʒodes, Jms.20.   (O.E. *god, gen. godes*.)

god, *adj. s.* or *sb.;* good, *M*.119, 247; *T*.394, 428, 442.   (O.E. *gōd*.)

god, *sb.;* property, goods, *T*.415, 634.   (O.E. *gōd*.)

godeliche, *adj. s.;* goodly, *M*.343.   (O.E. *gōdlīc*.)

godnesse, *sb.;* goodness, *Sp*.46.   (O.E. *gōdnes*.)

gold, *sb.;* gold, *M*.177, 181, etc.; *ʒold, Jms*.102; *glod, M*.102; *golde,
   dat. s., M*.101; *ʒolde, Jms*.101.   (O.E. *gold*.)

gras, *sb.;* grass, *M*.103; *ʒras, Jms*.103.   (O.E. *gærs, græs*.)

grene, *adj. s.;* green, *M*.334; *Jms*.334.   (O.E. *grēne*.)

grennen, *vb. inf.;* grin, *T*.647.   (O.E. *grennian*.)

grewe, *pt. subj. s.;* were to grow, *M*.102; *ʒrepe, Jms*.102.   (O.E. *grōwan,
   pt. subj. s. grēowe*.)

gripen, *vb. inf.;* seize; *gripen to,* seize upon, *M*.149.   (O.E. *grīpan*.)

grith, *sb.;* security, *Sp*.87; *ʒriþ, Jms*.87.   (O.E. *griþ*.)

ʒan, *pt. s.;* began, *W*.13; *Jms*.13.   (O.E. *begann* or *ongann*.)

ʒe, *pro.;* ye, you, *W*.27; *Jms*.27; *M*.307, etc.   See *ʒu.*   (O.E. *gē*.)

ȝef, *imp. s.;* give, grant, *T*.576. (O.E. *giefan, imp. s. gif.*)

ȝif, *conj.;* if, *M*.138, etc.; *T*.352, etc. (O.E. *gif.*)

ȝin, see *gin.*

ȝodes, see *god.*

ȝold, ȝolde, see *gold.*

ȝras, see *gras.*

ȝrepe, see *grewe.*

ȝriþ, see *grith.*

ȝu, *pro.;* you, *W*.29; *Jms*.29; *T*.190. See ȝe. (O.E. *ȝē.*)

ȝuȝþe, ȝuþe, *sb.;* youth, *M*.127, 135. (O.E. *geogoð, iugoð.*)

ȝung, *adj. s.;* young, *T*.348; ȝunge, *T*.572. (O.E. *geong.*)

ȝure, *poss. pro.;* your, *W*.28; *Jms*.28, etc. (O.E. *ēower.*)

habbe, *pr. subj. s.;* may have, *M*.319; *Jms*.461; *hafe,* have, *M*.109. See *hapen.* (O.E. *habban, pr. subj. s. hæbbe.*)

hachte, for *ahte, sb.;* property, wealth, *T*.410; *haite, T*.624. (O.E. *æht.*)

hafe, see *habbe.*

haite, see *hachte.*

hapen, *vb. inf.;* have, *T*.363, 573; *hapit, pr. s., T*.433; *hauit, T*.653; *haueþ, M*.199, 263, etc.; *haueþh, M*.182; *hauest, pr. 2 s., M*.138, 176, etc.; *hauist, T*.376, 404; *hauedest, pt. 2 s., M*.218, 288; *haue, pr. subj. s., Jms*.87, 109; *Sp*.87; see *habbe, hafe; hauede, pt. subj. s., Jms*.100; *M*.98, 100; *haue, imp. s., M*.477; *hape, T*.453. (O.E. *habban.*)

he, *pro.;* she, *Jms*.340, 612; *T*.351, 352, etc. (O.E. *hēo.*)

helde, for *elde, sb.;* old man, *T*.573. (O.E. *eald,* old.)

helden, *vb. inf.;* hold, *Jms*.70, 409; *Sp*.70; *M*.132; *T*.579; *holden, T*.409; *helden, pp.,* restrained, *M*.311. (O.E. *healdan, pp. healden.*)

helder, for *elder, adj. comp.;* older, *T*.600. (O.E. *ieldra, yldra.*)

help, *sb.;* help, *T*.635. (O.E. *help.*)

hem, *pro.;* them, themselves, *W*.13; *Jms*.13; *M*.305. (O.E. *him, heom.*)

hen, *pro.;* him, *T*.631. (O.E. *hine.*)

henne, *adv.;* hence, *M*.166. (O.E. *heonan.*)

her, *sb.;* hair, *T*.538. (O.E. *hær.*)

her, *adv.;* here, *M*.129, 470; *T*.190. (O.E. *hēr.*)

her, for *er, conj.;* before, *T*.269; *adv., T*.379. (O.E. *ær.*)

here, *poss. pro.;* their, *W*.15; *Jms*.15. (O.E. *hiera, heora.*)

hereȝonȝ, *sb.;* invasion of an army, *Jms*.86; *Sp*.86. (O.E. *heregung.*)

heren, *vb. inf.;* hear, *W*.14; *Jms*.14, 418; *T*.418; *herest, pr. 2 s., M*.328. (O.E. *hīeran.*)

herliche, *adv.;* early, *T*.436. (O.E. *ærlīce.*)

herte, *sb.;* heart, *M*.219; *T*.540, 652, 653. (O.E. *heorte*.)

hes, for *he*, he, *as*, them; see *T*.100; *pro.; Jms*.100; *M*.100. (O.E. *as*, early Southern or Southeastern form. See *N.E.D.*, *his*, *hise*.)

heþen, *adv.;* hence, *M*.168, 482. (O.E. *heonan*.)

heure, see note to line 634.

hepere, for *euere*, *adv.;* ever, always, *T*.648. (O.E. *æfre*.)

hepit, *sb.;* head, *T*.390. (O.E. *hēafod*.)

hi, *pro.;* they, *W*.14, 15; *Jms*.14, 15, etc. (O.E. *hīe*, *hī*.)

hi, for *ic;* see *hic*.

hic, *pro.;* I, *T*.665; *hich*, *T*.535; *hi*, *T*.441. (O.E. *ic*.)

hid, *pro.;* see *hit*.

hid, *pp.;* hidden, *T*.410. (O.E. *hȳdan*, *pp. hȳdd* or *hȳded*.)

hie, *pro.;* she, *T*.353. (O.E. *hēo*, *hīe*.)

hille, see *ille*.

hime, *pro.;* him, *Jms*.106. (O.E. *him*.)

hin, *pro.;* him, *T*.582. (O.E. *hine*.)

hirde, *sb.;* shepherd, *W*.10; *Jms*.10. (O.E. *hierde*.)

hire, *pers.* and *poss. pro.;* her, *Jms*.266, 338; *M*.287, 338; *T*.266, 269, 430, 443, etc. (O.E. *hiere*, *hire*.)

his, *pr. s.;* is, *M*.227; *T*.276 (is it to him), 635, 641. (O.E. *is*.)

hise, *poss. pro.;* his, *M*.493. (O.E. *his*.)

hit, *pro.;* it, *M*.123, 169, 228; *T*.354; *hid*, *T*.433, 609. (O.E. *hit*.)

hoe, *pro.;* she, *M*.285, 289, 295, etc.; *ho*, *M*.291. (O.E. *hēo*.)

hokede, *adj. pl.;* hooked (thievish), *T*.389. (O.E. *hōcede*, curved.)

hoker, *sb.;* scorn, *T*.630. (O.E. *hōcor*.)

hokerfule, *adj. s.;* scornful, *T*.622; *hokerful*, *T*.629. (O.E. *hōcor*, scorn, *ful*, full.)

holden, see *helden*.

honden, *sb.;* hands, *T*.389. (O.E. *hond*, *hand*.)

hore, *adj.* as *sb.;* hoary-headed man, *T*.586. (O.E. *hār*.)

horeling, *sb.;* fornicator, *T*.663. (O.E. *hōre*, whore.)

horse, *dat. s.;* on a horse, *M*.343. (O.E. *hors*.)

hu, *interr. adv.;* how, *W*.15; *Jms*.15, 31, 69; *Sp*.31, 69. (O.E. *hū*.)

hue, *pro.;* she, *T*.425, 431, etc. (O.E. *hēo*, *hīe*.)

huge, *adj. s.;* great, huge, *T*.656, 668. (O.F. *ahuge*.)

hundt seuenti, *adj.;* seventy, *M*.99; *hunt-seuenti*, *Jms*.99. (O.E. *hund-seofontig*.)

hunȝer, *sb.;* famine, *Jms*.86; *Sp*.86. (O.E. *hungor*.)

hþanne, *conj.;* when, *M*.166, 168, 171, etc. (O.E. *hwonne*, *hwanne*.)

hþar so, *adv.;* wheresoever, *T*.402. (O.E. *swā hwǣr swā*.)

hƿat, *interr. pro.;* what, *Jms*.108. (O.E. *hƿæt.*)

hƿider so, *adv.;* whithersoever, *M*.498. (O.E. *swā hwider swā.*)

hƿile, *conj.;* while, *T*.529; *hƿiles, M*.200, 227, 475. (O.E. *ða hwīle ðe,* the while that, while.)

hwo, hƿo, *indef. pro.;* whoever, who, *Sp*.59; *M*.195, 199; *hƿo so,* whoso-ever, *Jms*.358; *M*.262. (O.E. *hwā.*)

hƿungman, error for *hჳungman, sb.;* young man, *M*.111. (O.E. *geong man.*)

ic, *pro.;* I, *Jms*.412; *ich, T*.190, 412, 457, etc. (O.E. *ic.*)

icƿeme, *pr. subj. s.;* may please, *Jms*.66; *Sp*.66. Evidently an error; see note to line 66. (O.E. *gecwēman.*)

idilscipe, *sb.;* idleness, *T*.347. (O.E. *īdel* plus *scipe.* Cf. *īdelness.*)

idrunken, *pp.;* drunk, *M*.263. (O.E. *gedruncen, pp.*)

ifel, *adj. s.;* evil, *Jms*.274. (O.E. *yfel.*)

iჳiuene, *pp.;* given, *M*.128. (O.E. *giefan, pp. giefen.*)

ihasted, for *i-ahteþ, pr. s.;* estimates, *T*. 271. (O.E. *ge-eahtian.*)

iheren, *vb. inf.;* hear, *M*.315. (O.E. *gehīeran.*)

ihud, *pp.;* hidden, *Jms*.410. (O.E. *gehȳdan, pp. gehȳdd.*)

ileuen, *vb. inf.;* believe, *T*.649. (O.E. *gelīefan.*)

iliche, *adv.;* alike, *T*.398. (O.E. *gelīce.*)

ille, *adj. s.;* ill, going wrong, *M*.284; *adv.,* severely, *Jms*.611; *T*.611; *hille, T*.616. (O.N. *illr* (*adj.*); *illa* (*adv.*).)

inne, *adv.;* within, inside, *M*.484. (O.E. *innan.*)

inoჳe, *adj. s.;* enough, *M*.177; *inoh, Jms*.411; *inoch, T*.411. (O.E. *genōge, genōh.*)

inoh, inoch, see *inoჳe.*

is, for *his, poss. pro.;* his, *M*.133, 468; *T*.275, 358, 361, 375, 390, 458, 573, 644, 652. (O.E. *his.*)

isait, *pp.;* said, *T*.433. (O.E. *gesecgan, pp. gesæd.*)

iscoten, *pp.;* shot, *T*.456. (O.E. *sceotan, pp. gescoten.*)

iuel, *adj. s.;* evil, *M*.274; *T*.274, 354 (difficult); *ipil, T*.662. See *ifel.* (O.E. *yfel.*)

iuele, *dat. s.;* evil, *M*.112, 119. (O.E. *yfel.*)

iuele, *adv.;* evilly, *M*.263; *T*.271, 277 (ill). (O.E. *yfele.*)

iwerche, *pr. subj. s.;* make, *M*.107; *ipurche, Jms*.107. (O.E. *gewyrcan.*)

ipil, see *iuel.*

iapraþed, *pp.;* angered, *T*.425. (O.E. *gewrāðian.*)

ipurche, see *iwerche.*

i-ƿurþen, *vb. inf.;* turn, become, *T*.518; *i-ƿurþe, pr. subj. s.,* may happen, *M*.500. (O.E. *geweorþan*).

keren, see note to line 624.

kinȝ, *sb.;* king, *W*.12, 18, etc.; *Jms*.12, 18, etc.; *T*.664. See *cing.* (O.E. *cyning, cyng.*)

kinne, *gen. pl.* (?); of (no) kinds, *M*.489. Cf. *cunne, T*.505. (O.E. *cynn, gen. pl. cynna.*)

knihtes, *gen. s.;* knight's, *Jms*.93; *cnihtes, Sp*.93. See *cniht.* (O.E. *cniht, gen. s. cnihtes.*)

lage, laȝe, *sb.;* law, *W*.8; *Jms*.8, 93; *Sp*.93; *lape, T*.557, 572. (O.E. *lagu* (*lag, lah*).)

laȝelice, *adj. pl.;* lawful, *Jms*.75; *laweliche, M*.75. (O.E. *lahlīc.*)

lagelice, laȝelice, *adv.;* lawfully, *Jms*.70; *Sp*.70. (O.E. *lahlīce.*)

laren, see *leren.*

lasse, þe lasse, *adv. expression;* the less, *M*.248. (O.E. *þē lǣs.*)

lasten, *vb. inf.;* last, endure, *M*.201; *T*.508; *laste, M*.476. (O.E. *lǣstan.*)

lat, see *leten.*

lape, laweliche, see *lage, laȝelice.*

leche, see *liche.*

lede, *sb.;* people, *Sp*.40; *T*.439 (among the people); *led, Jms*.439; *leden, pl., T*.571. (O.E. *lēod,* nation, people; *pl. lēode,* people.)

leden, *vb. inf.;* lead, guide, conduct, control, govern, *W*.16; *Jms*.16, 74, 407; *M*.74, 324, 488; *T*.407, 522. (O.E. *lǣdan.*)

lef, *adj. s.;* beloved, dear, *T*.189; *leue, T*.533, 637; *lepe, T*.620. (O.E. *lēof.*)

lefe, *sb.;* belief, trust, *M*.477. (O.E. (*ge*)*lēafa.*)

lengen, *vb. inf.;* prolong, *T*.514. (O.E. *lengan.*)

lengest, *adv. supl.;* longest, *M*.324. (O.E. *lengest.*)

leren, *vb. inf.;* teach, *Jms*.13; *T*.190, 523, 596 (learn); *laren, W*.13; *lere, pr. 1 s., T*.567; *lerit, pr. s., T*.348; *ler, imp. s., M*.228; *T*.391; *lere,* learn, *T*.599. (O.E. *lǣran.*)

lese, *adj. s.;* false, *T*.622. (O.E. *lēas.*)

lesen, *vb. inf.;* lose, *T*.390. (O.E. *lēosan.*)

lesing, *sb.;* lying, deception, *T*.630; *lesin*[*ge*], *T*.387. (O.E. *lēasung.*)

lest, *adv.;* least, *T*.609. (O.E. *lǣst, lǣsest.*)

leten, *vb. inf.;* abandon, give up, allow, let, *M*.147, 159, 172, etc.; *T*.515; *letest, pr. 2 s., M*.233; *lat, pr. s., Jms*.358; *T*.358; *imp. s., T*.573; *let, imp. s., M*.221; *T*.577; *let þe,* behave thyself, *T*.557; *letet,* for *let it,* disregard it, *T*.413. (O.E. *lǣtan.*)

lepe-bei, *adj. s.;* supple-jointed, pliable, *T*.651. (O.E. *leoðu-bīge.*)

leþen, for *leʒen, vb. inf.;* lie, deceive, *T*.392. (O.E. *lēogan.*)

leþere, *adj. pl.;* bad, *T*.349. (O.E. *lȳðre.*)

leue, leþe, see *lef.*

leuen, *vb. inf.;* believe, trust, *M*.325; *lef, imp. s., Jms*.413; *M*.174. (O.E. *gelīefan.*)

licen, *pr. subj. 2 pl.;* may please, *Sp*.43; *liceð, pr. s.,* pleases, *Jms*.413; *likeþ, M*.210, 222, 301; *liket, T*.413; *like, pr. subj. s., M*.114. (O.E. *līcian.*)

liche, *sb.;* body, *M*.258; *leche blod,* body blood, *M*.259. (O.E. *līc.*)

lif, *sb.;* life, *W*.15; *Jms*.15; *Sp*.44; *M*.146, 157, 160, etc.; *liues, gen. s.* with *þene, M*.155. (O.E. *līf.*)

lifen, *vb. inf.;* live, *M*.180. (O.E. *libban.*)

ligen, *vb. inf.;* lie, recline, *M*.254. (O.E. *licgan.*)

liʒen, *vb. inf.;* lie, deceive, *M*.156; *T*.629. (O.E. *lēogan.*)

liht, *sb.;* light, *M*.495. (O.E. *lēoht.*)

like, likeþ, see *licen.*

listeliche, *adv.;* cunningly, *T*.625. (O.E. *listelīce.*)

listis, *sb.;* arts, devices, *T*.597; *liste, dat. s.,* with skill, cunning, *M*.489. (O.E. *list.*)

litel, *adj. s.;* little, *M*.227; *littele, T*.639; *lutele, T*.516; *luttele, T*.641; *adv.,* little, for a little time, *litel, M*.255; *lutel, T*.508; *liten, M*.151. (O.E. *lītel, lȳtel.*)

liten, probably an error; see *litel.*

liþen, *vb. inf.;* listen, *W*.27; *Jms*.27. (Icel. *hlȳða.* Cf. O.E. *hlystan.*)

liues, see *lif.*

loage, loare, see *lore.*

locen, *vb. inf.;* see to it, observe, pay heed to, *Jms*.68, 94; *Sp*.68, 94; *loke, imp. s., T*.368, 370, 393. (O.E. *lōcian.*)

loke, see *locen.*

lond, *sb.;* land, *Jms*.69, 74, 85; *Sp*.69, 85; *M*.74; *T*.573, 578; *londe, dat. s.,* the country, *T*.401. (O.E. *lond, land.*)

lone, *sb.;* loan, gift, *M*.143, 493. (O.E. *lǣn.*)

long, *adj. s.;* tall, long, *T*.639; *lonke, T*.651; *longes, gen., M*.155; *adv.,* long, *longe, M*.470; *so longe,* as long as, *T*.626. (O.E. *long, lang* (*adj.*); *longe* (*adv.*).)

lonke, see *long.*

lore, *dat. s.;* lore, *T*.667; *loare, Jms*.65*; *loage, Sp*.65*. (O.E. *lār.*)

loð, *adj. s.;* hateful, hostile, loathly, *T*.387; *loþe,* as *sb.,* the hostile one, *M*.323. (O.E. *lāð.*)

louerd, *sb.;* the Lord, lord, *W*.28; *Jms*.28, 361; *Sp*.44; *M*.170, 492; *T*.361, 550; *louird, gen. s., T*.644. (O.E. *hlāford.*)

lopien, *vb. inf.;* love, *T.*558, 570; *luueþ, pr. s., M.*158; *luuede, pt. s., W.*20; *luvede, Jms.*20; *luuiend,* for *luuien, pr. subj. 2 pl., Sp.*43; *luuiende, pr. pt., Sp.*40. (O.E. *lufian.*)

lude, *adv.;* aloud; *lude and stille,* aloud and in silence, i.e., under all circumstances, *T.*429. (O.E. *hlūde.*)

luden, *sb.;* noises, *T.*646. (O.E. *hlȳd.*)

lusninde, *pr. pt.;* listening (eaves-dropping), *T.*605, 613. (O.E. *hlysnan, pr. pt. hlysnende.*)

lusten, *vb. inf.;* listen to, pay attention to, *W.*28; *Jms.*28; *lust, imp. s., T.*188. (O.E. *hlystan.*)

lustlike, *adv.;* eagerly, *T.*188. (O.E. *lustlīce.*)

luþere, *adj.* or *sb.;* evil, evil man, *T.*388, 605, 610, 613. See *leþere.* (O.E. *lȳðre.*)

luu- and **luv-** forms, see *lopien.*

madmes, *sb.;* treasures, *M.*150, 176; *T.*505. (O.E. *māþum.*)

mai, *pr. s.;* may, *Jms.*63; *Sp.*63, etc.; *mei, M.*296. (O.E. *magan, pr. s. mæg.*)

maist, *pr. 2 s.;* mayst, *T.*374, 399. (O.E. *magan.*)

maister, *sb.;* master, *Sp.*52; *T.*359, 644; *master, Jms.* 359. (O.F. *maistre.*)

maken, *vb. inf.;* make, *T.*279, 646; *makeþ, pr. s., M.*467; *makede, pt. s., M.*497. (O.E. *macian, pt. s. macode.*)

mani, *adj. s.;* many a, *Jms.*334, 337; *M.*153, 181, etc.; *indef. pro., M.*329; *manni, adj. s., M.*337; *moni, T.*270, 363, etc.; *indef. pro., T.*666; *manie, adj. pl.,* many, *W.*2; *Jms.*2; *M.*176; *T.*448. (O.E. *monig, manig.*)

mannes, *gen. s.;* man's, *M.*80, 228, 326; *monnis, T.*452; *manne, gen. pl., Sp.*51; *dat. pl., M.*330. (O.E. *mon(n), man(n).*)

maþeleþ, *pr. s.;* speaks, *M.*312. (O.E. *maþelian, pr. s. maþelaþ.*)

me, *indef. pro.;* one, man, *M.*237, 320, 323; *T.*600, 650. (O.E. *mon(n), man(n).*)

medes, *sb.;* meadows, *Jms.*90; *Sp.*90. (O.E. *mǣd.*)

mei, see *mai.*

melten, *vb. inf.;* melt, *T.*506. (O.E. *meltan, myltan.*)

mestes, for *metes, pr. 2 s.;* meetest, *T.*574. (O.E. *mētan.*)

mi, *poss. pro.;* my, mine, *T.*548, 640; *min, T.*533, 537, etc. (O.E. *mīn.*)

michte, michten, see *miht.*

mid, *prep.;* with, *Jms.*75, 101; *M.*75, 101, etc.; *mide* (following object), *M.*195, *T.*370; *mit, T.*579. (O.E. *mid.*)

middellert, *sb.;* earth, *T.*510. (O.E. *middaneard, middangeard.*)

miht, *pr. 2 s.;* canst, mayst, *M.*215, 490; *mith, M.*217; *mitht, T.*607; *mist, T.*513, 578, 596, etc.; *michte, pt. s., T.*443; *mihten, pt. 2 pl., Jms.*31; *michten, Sp.*31; *mihten, pt. pl., W.*14; *Jms.*14. (O.E. *magan, pr. 2 s. miht, pt. s. mihte, pt. pl. mihton.*)

mihte, *sb.;* might, strength, *M.*468; *misten, pl.,* powers, *T.*556. (O.E. *meaht, miht.*)

milde, *adj. s.;* mild, *Sp.*52. (O.E. *milde.*)

mildeliche, *adv.;* mildly, *Sp.*37. (O.E. *mildelīce.*)

min, see *mi.*

minde, *adj. s.;* present to one's thought, *T.*560. See *mind, adj. obs. 1, N.E.D.* (O.E. *gemynde.*)

mist, misten, see *miht, mihte.*

mit, see *mid.*

mith, mitht, see *miht.*

mod, *sb.;* mood, courage, attitude of mind, *M.*299; *T.*635, 427 (fit of anger). (O.E. *mōd.*)

moder, *sb.;* mother, *T.*357. (O.E. *mōdor.*)

mon, *sb.;* man, *T.*270, etc.; in apposition with *þu, T.*509; *monnis,* see *mannes.* (O.E. *mon(n), man(n).*)

moneȝen, *vb. inf.;* mention, *T.*419; *muniȝen, Jms.* 419. (O.E. *manian.*)

moni, see *mani.*

mor, *adj.* as *sb.;* more, *M.*218; *more, M.*313. (O.E. *mā.*)

moreuin, to moreuin, *adv.;* to-morrow, *T.*377. (O.E. *morgen.*)

morȝen, *sb.* as *adj.;* morning, *M.*260. (O.E. *morgen.*)

mote, *pr. subj. s.;* may, *M.*201; *T.*645. (O.E. *mōtan, pr. subj. s. mōte.*)

mopen, *vb. inf.;* mow, *Jms.*79, 90; *mowen, Sp.*90; *M.*79. (O.E. *māwan.*)

mucheles, *adv. gen.;* much, *M.*261. (O.E. *micel.*)

muȝe, *pr. subj. 2 s.;* may, *M.*476; *pr. subj. s.,* may, can, *M.*131, 163; *pr. 1 pl., T.*524. (O.E. *magan, pr. subj. s. mæge.*)

multeplien, *vb. inf.;* multiply, *T.*634. (O.F. *multiplier.*)

mune, *pr. 1 s.;* admonish, *Sp.*37. (O.E. *manian.*)

muniȝen, see *moneȝen.*

murhþe, *sb.;* mirth, joy, *M.*496. (O.E. *myrgþ.*)

mused, *pr. s.;* mouseth, *T.*356. (Verb formed from O.E. *mūs,* mouse.)

muþ, *sb.;* mouth, *M.*312, 329; *muþe, dat. s., Jms.*419; *T.*419. (O.E. *mūð.*)

nahtest, *pt. 2 s.;* hadst not, *M.*242; *nepedest, T.*383. (O.E. *næbban.*)

narruliche, *adv.;* narrowly, *T.*407; *narplice, Jms.*407. (O.E. *nearolīce, nearulīce.*)

nauid, *pr. s.;* has not, *T*.461. See *nahtest.* (O.E. *næbban.*)

ne, *conj.;* nor. (O.E. *nē.*)

ne, *adv.;* not, *Sp*.57, etc. (O.E. *ne.*)

nede, *dat. s.;* need, time of need, *T*.394; *nude, M*.345; *neden, dat. pl.,* *T*.373. (O.E. *nēod.*)

nefre, *adv.;* never, *Jms*.265; *M*.111, 140, etc.; *neuer, T*.360, etc.; *neuere,* *M*.331; *T*.446, 450, etc. (O.E. *næfre.*)

nei, *prep.;* near, *T*.642; *adv.,* nigh, nearly, *T*.541. (O.E. *nēah, nēh.*)

neuer, neuere, see *nefre.*

nepe, *adj. pl.;* new, *T*.451. (O.E. *nīwe, nēowe.*)

nepedest, see *nahtest.*

nexte, *adj.* as *sb.;* neighbor or nearest relative, *T*.393. (O.E. *nexsta, nexta.*)

niht, ale niht, *adv. expression;* all night, *M*.254. (O.E. *niht.*)

nim, *imp. s.;* take, *T*.632. (O.E. *niman.*)

nis, for *ne is,* is not, *M*.142, 161. (O.E. *nis.*)

no, *adj. s.;* no; *no þing,* nothing, *T*.654. (O.E. *nān.*)

no, *conj.;* nor, *M*.479. (O.E. *nē.*)

nocht, see *noht.*

noht, *indef. pro.;* nothing, nought, *Sp*.58; *M*.178, 296; *nocht, T*.506; *nout, T*.628; *noht, adv.,* not, in no degree, *Jms*.105; *M*.174, 204; *nocht, M*.105; *T*.441; *noth, T*.423; *nout, T*.665. (O.E. *nā-wiht,* *nōht.*)

noman, *indef. pro.;* no one, *M*.248. (O.E. *nān,* no, *mon,* man.)

non, *adj. s.;* no, *Jms*.267; *M*.142; *T*.267; *none, M*.477; *T*.514; *pl.,* *M*.489; *nones, gen., T*.452; *non, indef. pro., Jms*.461, *T*.461, 642; *none,* *M*.480. (O.E. *nān.*)

not, *pr. s.;* knows not, *M*.165. (O.E. *nytan, pr. s. nāt.*)

noth, nout, see *noht.*

nu, *adv.;* now, *W*.27; *Jms*.27; *T*.534. (O.E. *nū.*)

nude, see *nede.*

o, *indef. art.;* a, *Jms*.98. (O.E. *ān,* one.)

o, for *of, prep.;* of, *M*.299. (O.E. *of.*)

o, for *on, prep.;* in, *Jms*.65*; *Sp*.65*; *T*.569. (O.E. *on.*)

of, *prep.;* from, of, *Jms*.86, 106; *Sp*.86; *M*.106; *T*.581. (O.E. *of.*)

of-reden, *vb. inf.;* surpass in counsel, *T*.601. (O.E. *ofrædan.*)

of-riden, *vb. inf.;* outride, *T*.600. (O.E. *ofrīdan.*)

ofte, *adv.;* often, *M*.304; *T*.272, 356, etc.; *ofter, adv. comp., T*.428. (O.E. *oft, comp. oftor.*)

ofþincheþ, *pr. s.;* it displeaseth, it repenteth, *Jms*.420; *of-þinket, T*.420. (O.E. *ofþyncan.*)

oʒen, *adj. s.;* own, *M*.160, 234, 494; *oʒe, M*.308; *oʒene, M*.146; *owen, M*.81. (O.E. *āgen.*)

oliue, *adv.;* in life, *T*.276. (O.E. *on līfe.*)

on, *num.;* one, *T*.627. (O.E. *ān.*)

one, *adj. s.;* alone, *Sp.*45–55; *M*.169; *T*.378. (O.E. *āna.*)

one, for *on a* or *on; prep.;* in a, in, *T*.516, 591. Cf. *J*.395. (O.E. *on.*)

oni, *adj. s.;* any, *T*.447. (O.E. *ænig.*)

onsuerren, *vb. inf.;* answer, *T*.625. (O.E. *ondswarian.*)

op, *prep.;* upon, *M*.344. (O.E. *uppon.*)

orgul prude, *sb.;* great pride, *T*.347. (O.E. *orgel,* pride; *prūt,* pride. Cf. O.F. *orgoill, orguill.*)

oþer, oþir, *adj. s.* or *pl.;* other, *T*.544, 559; *adv.,* otherwise, *T*.435, 629; *oþere, indef. pro.,* others, *T*.444. (O.E. *ōðer.*)

oþer, *conj.;* or, *T*.426, 575. (O.E. *oððe.*)

oþer-þile, *adv.;* sometimes, *T*.431. (O.E. *oþerhwīle.*)

ouer, *prep.;* over, *Sp.*46, etc.; *oþer, T*.559. (O.E. *ofer.*)

ouergangen, *vb. inf.;* transgress, *M*.240. (O.E. *ofergangan.*)

ouergoþ, *pr. s.;* surpasses, *M*.193. (O.E. *ofergān, pr. s. ofergǣþ.*)

ouer-mukil, *adv.;* over-much, *T*.392. (O.E. *ofer-micel.*)

owen, see *oʒen.*

oþer, see *ouer.*

oþerlde, for *on þerlde;* in the world, on earth, *T*.395. (O.E. *on weorulde* or *worulde.*)

plopes, *sb.;* ploughs, *Jms.*91; *Sp.*91. (O.E. *plōh.*)

pouere, *adj.* as *sb.;* poor, *T*.397. (O.F. *povre.*)

prude, *sb.;* pride, *T*.347. (O.E. *prūt (sb.).)*

prude, *adj. pl.;* proud, *W*.5; *Jms.*5. (O.E. *prūt (adj.).)*

pruden, *vb. inf.;* show (himself) proudly, *T*.645. (O.E. *prūtian.*)

quad, *pt. s.;* quoth, *T*.187, 264, etc. (O.E. *cpeþan, pt. s. cpæþ.*)

quemen, *vb. inf.;* please, *T*.650. (O.E. *cwēman.*)

quene, *gen. s.;* woman's, *T*.440. (O.E. *cwēn, gen. s. cwēne.*)

quet, for *qued, sb.;* bad man, *T*.661. (O.E. *cwead.*)

red, *sb.;* counsel, advice, *Jms.*440; *T*.437, 440, 662, etc.; *reid, T*.434; *reides, pl., T*.599. (O.E. *ræd.*)

rede, *adj. s.;* red, red-haired, *Jms.*101; *M*.101; *T*.661; *red, T*.639. (O.E. *rēad.*)

reden, *vb. inf.;* advise, *T*.372; *rede, pr. subj. s., T*.561. (O.E. *rædan.*)

rei, *adj. s.;* fierce, passionate, *T.*641, 652. (O.E. *hrēoh.*)

reid, reides, see *red.*

reme, *adj. s.;* empty, unoccupied, *T.*576; doubtless a scribal error for *rume.* Skeat (pp. 67–68) tries to explain as *vb.:* "do thou permit him to clear the way, i.e., to have plenty of room." The context indicates an *adj.* (O.E. *rūm.*)

rere, *vb. inf.;* raise, procure, *T.*362. (O.E. *rǣran.*)

repen, *vb. inf.;* rue, *M.*236. (O.E. *hrēowan.*)

riche, *adj. s.;* rich, *Sp.*56; as *sb.*, *T.*397. (O.E. *rīce.*)

rid, *imp. s.;* ride, *M.*206. (O.E. *rīdan.*)

riht, *sb.;* right, justice, *Jms.*77; *M.*77. (O.E. *riht.*)

riht, *adj. s.;* righteous, *Jms.*63; *Sp.*63. (O.E. *riht.*)

riht-wis, *adj. s.;* righteous, *Sp.*55. (O.E. *rihtwīs.*)

rimen, *vb. inf.;* depart, make room, *M.*166. (O.E. *rȳman.*)

risten, for *rihten, vb. inf.;* right, *T.*555. (O.E. *rihtan.*)

rowen, *vb. inf.;* row, *M.*123. (O.E. *rōwan.*)

sadel boȝe, *dat. s.;* saddle bow, *M.*205. (O.E. *sadel-boga.*)

saȝe, *sb.;* proverb, saw, *T.*385. (O.E. *sagu.*)

saȝin, *vb. inf.;* say, tell, *T.*590; *saȝe, pr. 1 s.*, *T.*441; *saiȝe, T.*412; *sait, pr. s.*, *T.*458; *saide, pt. s.*, *T.*526; *sai, imp. s..* *M.*499; *said, pp., T.*439. See *sege.* (O.E. *secgan.*)

sai- forms, see *saȝin.*

sal, *pr. s.;* shall, *M.*79, 156, etc.; *scal, Sp.*57; *M.*159, 166, etc.; *scall, Jms.*79; *salt, pr. 2 s.*, *T.*265, 515, etc. See *scullen.* (O.E. *sculan, pr. s. sceal.*)

Salomon, *pr. n.;* Solomon, *T.*433, 526, 527.

salt, *sb.;* salt, *M.*257. (O.E. *sealt, salt.*)

samne, *vb. inf.;* unite, *Jms.*34; *Sp.*34. (O.E. *samnian.*)

sapen, *pp.;* shaped, destined, *M.*121. (O.E. *scieppan.*)

scal, scall, see *sal.*

scene, *adj. s.;* beautiful, *Jms.*339; *M.*339. (O.E. *scīene.*)

scete, *sb.;* sheet, *Jms.*339; *M.*339. (O.E. *scēat.*)

scold, *sb.;* scold, *T.*447; *scolde, T.*664. (O. N. *skāld.* See *scold, N.E.D.*)

scolde, scollen, etc., see *scullen.*

scondes, *gen. s.;* of shame, *Jms.*340; *M.*340. (O.E. *scand.*)

scullen, *pr. 1 pl.;* shall, *M.*172; *sullen, M.*145; *sulen, T.*542; *scollen, pr. pl.*, *M.*314; *sullen, M.*148; *sulen, T.*506, 570; *scolde, pt. s.*, *M.*289, 313; *T.*351; *sholde, M.*111, etc.; *sulde, T.*459; *scolden, pt. pl.*, *W.*16; *Jms.*16. (O.E. *sculan, pt. s. sceolde, scolde.*)

sedes, *sb.;* seeds, *Jms*.89; *Sp*.89. (O.E. *sēd*.)

se-flode, *dat. s.;* sea flood, *M*.124, 175. (O.E. *sǣ flod*.)

sege, *vb. inf.;* say, tell, speak, *M*.215, 217; *sigen*, *T*.535; *seȝȝe*, *pr. 1 s.*, *Jms*.412; *sige*, *T*.665; *seist*, *pr. 2 s.*, *M*.212; *seiþ*, *pr. s.*, *Jms*.439; *seȝeþ*, *M*.321; *seiþ*, *pr. s.* as *fut.*, *M*.207; *seiȝe*, *pr. subj. 2 s.*, *M*.283, 300; *seie*, *imp. s.*, *M*.205; *seiȝe*, *M*.204. (O.E. *secgan*.)

seȝe, *pt. subj. s.;* should see, *M*.285. (O.E. *sēon*.)

seie, seiȝe, seist, seiþ, see *sege*.

seiþin, see *siþen*.

selden, *adv.;* seldom, *T*.364; *selde*, *T*.652. (O.E. *seldan*.)

sele, *dat. s.*, happiness, *T*.364. (O.E. *sǣl*.)

seli, *adj. s.;* happy, *T*.400. (O.E. *gesǣlig*.)

selliche, *adv.;* wonderfully, *T*.363. (O.E. *sellīce*.)

selþe, *sb.;* good fortune, *T*.386. (O.E. *sǣlþ*.)

selue, selpe, *ref. pro.* when combined with *pers. pro.;* -self, *Jms*.461; *M*.476, 491; *T*.461; self, *M*.466; *seluen, selpen, pl.*, *T*.521, 595, etc. (O.E. *self*.)

sendeþ, *pr. s.;* is, *M*.195. (Cf. O.E. *sindon*, they are.)

sendeþ, *pr. s.;* sendeth, *Jms*.405; *senden*, *T*.405. (O.E. *sendan*.)

seruȝe, see *sorȝe*.

sete, seten, see *sitten*.

sete, *sb.;* seat, *T*.588. (O.N. *sǣti*.)

sholde, see *scullen*.

sibbe, *adj. pl.;* related, *M*.304. (O.E. *gesib(b)*.)

sicer, see *siker*.

Sifforde, *pr. n., dat.;* Siford, *Domesday Book* name for Shefford, Berkshire; *W*.1; *Jms*.1.

sige, sigen, see *sege*.

siker, *adv.;* securely, certainly, *M*.194; *T*.412; *sicer*, *Jms*.412. (O.E. *sicor*.)

sikerliche, *adv.;* safely, securely, *T*.399. (O.E. *sicerlīce*.)

singe, *vb. inf.;* sing, utter, *M*.328; *singinde, pr. pt.*, *M*.206. (O.E. *singan*, *pr. pt. singende*.)

sitten, *vb. inf.;* sit, *Jms*.417; *M*.194; *sittin*, *T*.400; *sitthest, pr. 2 s.*, *T*.585; *seten, pt. pl.*, *W*.1; *Jms*.2; *site, imp. s.*, *T*.534; *sete*, *T*.594. (O.E. *sittan*.)

siþen, *adv.;* afterwards, *T*.582; *seiþin*, *T*.594. (O.E. *siðð an*.)

sixst, *pr. 2 s.;* seest, *T*.586. (O.E. *sēon, pr. 2 s. siehst*.)

slep, *sb.;* sleep, *M*.260. (O.E. *slǣp*.)

slepen, *vb. inf.;* sleep, *M*.255. (O.E. *slǣpan*.)

slit, *pr. s.;* slides, *T.*659.   (O.E. *slīdan.*)

smerten, *vb. inf.;* smart, *T.*583; *smerteþ, pr. s., T.*654.   (O.E. *smeortan.*)

so, *conj.* or *adv.;* so, as, *M.*103; *T.*523, 567.   (O.E. *swā.*)

sone, *sb.;* son, *T.*533, 537, 547, etc.; *sune, dat. s., M.*479.   (O.E. *sunu, dat. s. suna.*)

sone, *adv.;* soon, *T.*456, 591, 589 (quickly).   (O.E. *sōna.*)

sor, *sb.;* affliction, *M.*217.   (O.E. *sār.*)

sore, *adv.;* sorely, *M.*236.   (O.E. *sāre.*)

sorӡe, *sb.;* sorrow, care, *M.*211, 256; *soreӡe, Jms.*411; *soriӡe, M.*203; *seruӡe, T.*438; *sorwe, M.*123.   (O.E. *sorg.*)

soriӡe, soreӡe, sorwe, see *sorӡe.*

sot, *sb.;* fool, *T.*580; *sottis, gen. s., T.*456.   (O.E. *sot.*)

soþe, *sb.;* truth, sooth, *T.*628.   (O.E. *sōð.*)

soþe, *adj. pl.;* true, *T.*536.   (O.E. *sōð.*)

soule, *sb.;* soul, *Jms.*33; *Sp.*33; *M.*184.   (O.E. *sāwol, sāwl.*)

sopen, *vb. inf.;* sow, *Jms.*89; *Sp.*89; *sopeþ, pr. s., Jms.*78; *M.*78; *sopen, pp., Jms.*100; *M.*100.   (O.E. *sāwan.*)

speche, *sb.;* speech, *W.*22; *Jms.*22; *M.*326; *T.*569.   (O.E. *spræc.*)

stable, *adj. s.;* stable, steadfast, *T.*632.   (O.F. *estable.*)

stede, *sb.;* steed, *M.*344.   (O.E. *stēda.*)

stelin, *vb. inf.;* steal, *T.*624.   (O.E. *stelan.*)

sternen, for *steren, vb. inf.;* guide, steer, *M.*491.   (O.E. *stīeran.*)

sticke, *sb.;* stick, *T.*656.   (O.E. *sticca.*)

stille, *adj. s.;* still, *T.*459, 615; *adv.,* quietly, in silence, *Jms.*612; *M.*219; *T.*429, 612.   (O.E. *stille.*)

ston, *sb.;* stone, *Jms.*108; *M.*108; *T.*656.   (O.E. *stān.*)

stonden, *vb. inf.;* stand, *T.*587.   (O.E. *stondan, standan.*)

stondes, see *stunde.*

stoni, *adj. s.;* stony, *T.*653.   (O.E. *stānig.*)

stren, *sb.;* acquisition, *M.*142.   (O.E. *(ge)strēon.*)

strengþe, *sb.;* strength, *M.*490.   (O.E. *strengðu.*)

stretes, *sb.;* streets, *T.*575.   (O.E. *stræt.*)

stronӡ, *adj. s.;* strong, *W.*18; *Jms.*18.   (O.E. *strong, strang.*)

stunde, *dat. s.;* hour, *T.*516; *stondes, gen. s., T.*341.   (O.E. *stund.*)

sug, corruption of *swich* or *swuch* ? *adj. s.;* such, *T.*635.   (O.E. *swilc.*)

suhþ, see *sukeþ.*

sukeþ, *pr. s.;* sucketh, *M.*258; *suhþ, M.*256.   (O.E. *sūcan.*)

sulde, sullen, sulen, see *scullen.*

spich, see *spilch.*

spift, *adj. s.;* quick, swift, *M.*294.   (O.E. *swift.*)

spilch, *adj. s.;* such, *M*.215, 217; *spich, T*.414; *spulc, Jms*.414.   (O.E. *swilc.*)

swinch, possibly an error for *swich,* such, such as, *M*.128.   (O.E. *swilc.*)

swinken, *vb. inf.;* work, *M*.125.   (O.E. *swincan.*)

spiðe, spiþe, *adv.;* very, *W*.18; *Jms*.18; *M*.136; *to spiþe,* too much, *M*.174; *T*.423; *spuðe, W*.8; *Jms*.8.   (O.E. *swiðe.*)

spo, *conj.* or *adv.;* so, as, *W*.14; *Jms*.14, 103; *T*.353, 526, 533.   (O.E. *swā.*)

spoti, *adj. s.;* sweaty, *T*.352.   (O.E. *swātig.*)

spulc, see *spilch.*

tahte, *pt. s.;* taught, *M*.238; *taite, T*.593.   (O.E. *tǣcan, pt. s. tǣhte.*)

taite, see *tahte.*

tales, *sb.;* tales, *T*.448.   (O.E. *talu.*)

te, *def. art.;* the, *Jms*.78, 87, etc.; *Sp*.87; *M*.76, 102, etc.   (O.E. *ðē.*)

te, *pro.;* thou, thee, *M*.206, 209, 216, etc.   (O.E. *ðū, ðē.*)

tellen, *vb. inf.;* tell, account, *T*.451; *tellit,* for *telle it, pr. 1 s., T*.628; *telle, T*.457.   (O.E. *tellan.*)

ten, *vb. inf.;* show, conduct, *T*.643.   (O.E. *tēon.*)

tene, *sb.;* sorrow, *T*.363.   (O.E. *tēona.*)

ter, see note to line 355.

the, *rel. pro.;* which, that, *Sp*.36.   (O.E. *ðe.*)

tideþ, *pr. s.;* happens, *M*.469.   (O.E. *tīdan.*)

tidinges, *sb.;* tidings, *T*.451.   (Late O.E. *tidung.*)

to, *adv.;* too, *M*.294; *T*.446, 453.   (O.E. *tō.*)

to-delen, *vb. inf.;* separate, *T*.542.   (O.E. *tōdǣlan.*)

tresten, *vb. inf.;* trust, *T*.374.   (O.N. *treysta.* Cf. O.E. *trūwian.*)

troþþe, *sb.;* truth, *T*.375.   (O.E. *trēowð.*)

tu, *pro.;* thou, *M*.218, 221, etc.   (O.E. *ðū.*)

tuenti, *num.;* twenty, *T*.627.   (O.E. *twēntig.*)

tune, *dat. s.;* town, *to tune,* idiom for *among us, M*.463.   (O.E. *tūn.*)

tunȝe, *sb.;* tongue, *Jms*.460; *M*.294; *tunke, T*.460.   (O.E. *tunge.*)

þ, symbol for *þat, Jms*.274, 418.

þad, see *þat.*

þanne, *conj.;* than, *M*.244, 313; *T*.428; when, *M*.118, 144, 157, 229, 235, 482; *T*.425, 459, 609.   (O.E. *þonne, þænne.*)

þanne, *adv.;* then, *M*.135, 148, etc.; *T*.380, 399, etc.   (O.E. *þonne, þænne.*)

þar after, *adv.;* thereafter, *M*.79.   (O.E. *þēr-æfter.*)

þarf, *pr. s.;* ought, need, *M*.154, 248, 318.   (O.E. *þurfan, pr. s. þearf*.)

þas þe, *adv. expression;* on that account, *M*.232.   (O.E. ðæs ðe.)

þat, *rel. pro.;* who, which, that, *W*.24; *Jms*.24, etc.; *þath, M*.121, 208; *þad, T*.437, 443, etc.; that which, *M*.309, 318, 500; *þath, M*.154. (O.E. *þæt.*)

þat, *dem. pro.;* that, *M*.74.   (O.E. *þæt.*)

þat, *conj.;* that, so that, *M*.209, etc.; *þad, T*.418; *þat ne,* but that, *M*.291.   (O.E. *þæt.*)

þau, *conj.;* though, *T*.509, 612, 615.   (O.E. *þeah.*)

þe, *def. art.;* the.   (O.E. ðē.)

þe, *rel. pro.;* who, which.   (O.E. ðe.)

þe, *dem. pro.;* those, *M*.73.   (O.E. ðā.)

þe, *pers. pro.;* thee, *M*.174, 285, 291, etc.   (O.E. ðē.)

þef, *sb.;* thief, *T*.663.   (O.E. ðēof.)

þeih, *conj.;* though, *Jms*.461.   (O.E. *þeah.*)

þeine, *pr. subj. 2 s.;* serve, *T*.368.   (O.E. *þegnian, þēnian*.)

þeines, *sb.;* thanes, *W*.2; *Jms*.2.   (O.E. *þegn.*)

þen, *conj.;* when, *T*.421, 432, 614, 618.   (O.E. *þonne, þænne*.)

þen, *acc. masc. s.;* the, *T*.389, 530, 586, 605, 622.   (O.E. ðone, ðane.)

þenchen, *vb. inf.;* think, plan, *T*.350; *þencheþ, pr. s., Jms*.421; ðenkeþ (corrected text), *Sp*.60; *þenked, T*.421; *þeng, imp. s., T*.406.   (O.E. *þencan.*)

þeng, see *þenchen.*

þenne, *conj.;* than, *T*.601; *adv.,* then, *T*.378, 521, etc.   (O.E. *þonne, þænne*.)

þer, *conj.;* where, *M*.320; *T*.531; *þere, Jms*.410; *adv.,* there, *W*.7; *Jms*.7, 411; *M*.251; *T*.411.   (O.E. *þǣr.*)

þer after, *adv.;* thereafter, *Jms*.79.   (O.E. *þǣr-æfter.*)

þer fro, *adv.;* therefrom, *M*.145.   (O.E. *þǣr from (fram).*)

þer-inne, *adv.;* therein, *T*.512.   (O.E. *þǣr-inne.*)

þer-mide, *adv.;* therewith, *T*.582.   (O.E. *þǣr-mid.*)

þer-to, *adv.;* thereto, *M*.230; *T*.589.   (O.E. *þǣr-tō.*)

þeþes, *sb.;* habits, manners, *M*.228; *T*.349; virtues, *T*.536; *þeues, T*.597; *þeuues,* good services, *T*.369.   (O.E. *þēaw.*)

þeþ[t]it, *pr. s.;* yells, howls, *T*.658.   See note.   (O.E. *þeotan.*)

þi, þin, þine, *poss. pro.;* thy, thine.   (O.E. ðīn.)

þing, *sb.;* thing, *T*.442, 654; *þinge, dat. s.,* for anything, *M*.290; *þinȝes, pl., W*.30; *Jms*.30; *M*.327; *þinke, dat. pl., T*.559.   (O.E. *þing.*)

þis, *dem. pro.;* this, *Jms*.93, etc.   (O.E. ðis.)

þisse, *dem. adj.;* this, *M*.139.   (O.E. ðisse.)

þo, *dem. pro.;* those, *Jms.*73; *M.*478.   (O.E. *ðā.*)

þo, þoch, see *þoh.*

þochte, *pt. subj. s.;* would think, *T.*353; *þoht, pp.,* thought, *M.*303.
(O.E. *þencan, pp.* (*ge*)*þōht.*)

þoh, *conj.;* though, *Jms.*98; *M.*98, 115, etc.; *þo, M.*113; *þoh, adv.,* nevertheless, *Jms.*340; *M.*340; *þoch, T.*354.   (O.E. *þēah.*)

þonke, *imp. s.;* thank, *M.*492.   (O.E. *þancian.*)

þonkes, *sb.;* thoughts, *M.*302.   (O.E. *þonc, þanc.*)

þu, *pro.;* thou, *M.*138, 140, etc.   (O.E. *ðū.*)

þur, þurch, see *þurh.*

þurh, *prep.;* through, *M.*183; *þur, M.*258; *þurch, T.*385, etc.; *þuru,*
*T.*630, 667; *þuruh, T.*388.   (O.E. *þurh.*)

þuru, þuruh, see *þurh.*

unborn, *pp.;* unborn, *M.*243.   (O.E. *pp. unboren.*)

unc, *dual pro.;* us two, *T.*542.   (O.E. *unc.*)

unibeten, *pp.;* not beaten, *M.*244.   (O.E. *pp. bēaten* with prefix *un.*)

unkuþe, *adj. pl.;* strange, *M.*464.   (O.E. *uncūð.*)

un-muke, *adj. s.;* impatient, *M.*467.   (O.N. *miūk-r.*   Cf. Early M.E.
meoc.)

unpurð, *adj. s.;* worthless, *Jms.*97; *M.*345; *vnpurþ, T.*388; *un-wurh,*
*M.*97.   (O.E. *unweorð.*)

uole, *pr. s.;* will, *T.*626, 627.   (O.E. *willan.*)

uor, *prep.;* for, *Jms.*85, 267; *conj., Jms.*108, 439.   (O.E. *for.*)

up-Breiden, *vb. inf.;* upbraid, *M.*291.   (O.E. *upbregdan.*)

up-helden, *vb. inf.;* uphold, sustain, *M.*164.   (O.E. *up*(*þ*)*healdan.*)

uppe, *prep.;* upon, *M.*175.   (O.E. *uppon.*).

ure, *poss. pro.;* our, *M.*146, 148, etc.; *T.*522; *pro., gen. pl.,* of us,
*Jms.*92; *Sp.*92.   (O.E. *ūre.*)

ut, *adv.;* out, *T.*658.   (O.E. *ūt, ūte.*)

uten, *adv.;* outside, on the outside, *Jms.*334; *M.*334, 483.   (O.E. *ūtan.*)

vimmon, see *pimman.*

vn-drunken, *pp.;* not drunk, sober, *M.*246.   (O.E. *pp. undruncen.*)

vnfoldit, for *umfoldiþ, pr. s.;* embraces, *T.*618.   (O.E. *fealdan* with prefix *ymb.*   Skeat (glossary) says compare *ymbclyppan.*)

vniselþe, *dat. s.;* misfortune, *M.*126.   (O.E. *unsǣlð.*)

vn-luden, *sb.;* unpleasant noises, *T.*648.   (O.E. *hlȳd* with prefix *un,*
meaning bad or unpleasant.   See Skeat, p. 70.)

vnpurþ, see *unpurþ.*

vretu, for *hure þu, imp. s.;* listen thou to, *T*.423.   (O.E. *hīeran.*)
vs, *pro.;* us, *M*.151.   (O.E. *ūs.*)

pan, *adj. s.;* wan, pale, *T*.539.   (O.E. *wonn, wann.*)
pane, *adj. s.;* wanting, *Sp*.57 (corrected text).   (O.E. *pana.*)
panne, *conj.;* when, *Jms*.421.   (O.E. *hwonne, hwanne.*)
par, *adj. s.;* wary, *W*.22; *T*.569; *pare, Jms*.22.   (O.E. *wær.*)
pe, *pro.;* we, *M*.171, 482; *T*.521, etc.   (O.E. *wē.*)
peie, *sb.;* way, path, *T*.576; *peis, pl., T*.575.   (O.E. *weg.*)
pel, *adv.;* well, very, *W*.18, 20; *Jms*.18, 20, 66, etc.; *M*.247, 467; *T*.436,
    528, etc.; *puel, M*.216.   (O.E. *wel.*)
pelden, *vb. inf.;* acquire, rule, govern, possess, *Jms*.32, 415; *Sp*.32;
    M.150, 233, 466; *T*.415; *peldest, pr. 2 s., M*.226; *T*.509; *poldest,*
    M.472; *welde, pr. subj. s., M*.115.   (O.E. *wealdan.*)
pele, see *pelþe.*
pele, pelle, see *pille, vb.*
pelþe, pelðe, *sb.;* wealth, prosperity, *Jms*.97, 104, 415; *M*.133, 138;
    T. 503, 511, etc.; *weleþe, M*.120; *wele, M*.97, 104; *pele, M*. 196,
    etc.   (O.E. *wela.*)
penden, *vb. inf.;* turn, depart, go, apply oneself, *M*.145, 168, 230; *T*.543,
    417 (come); *pent, pr. s., M*.197; *pende, pr. subj. 2 s.,* mayst go,
    M.498.   (O.E. *wendan.*)
penen, *vb. inf.;* expect, *T*.524; *pene, M*.154, 318; *penest, pr. 2 s.,*
    T.609; *peneþh, pr. s., M*.153; *peneþ, M*.317.   (O.E. *wēnan.*)
penes, for *pines, sb.;* friends, *T*.191.   (O.E. *wine.*)
pent, see *penden.*
peped, *pr. s.;* weepeth, *T*.427, 431.   (O.E. *wēpan.*)
per, *conj.;* where, *T*.410.   (O.E. *hwær.*)
perc, *sb.;* work, *W*.20; *Jms*.20.   (O.E. *weorc.*)
perd, *sb.;* crowd, quantity, *T*.656.   (O.E. *werod.*)
pere, *pt. 2 s.;* wast, *T*.379; *pt. subj. s.,* were, *Jms*.104; *M*.104, 186, 241,
    etc.; *puere, T*.352.   (O.E. *wære.*)
perie, *vb. inf.;* protect, *Jms*.85.   (O.E. *werian.*)
perld, *sb.;* world, *T*.529; *perldes, gen. s., Jms*.31; *M*.472; *T*.503; *werlds,*
    Sp.31; *werlde, dat. s., Sp*.59; *M*.129, 139; *T*.544.   (O.E. *weorold,*
    worold.)
persse, *adj. comp.;* worse, *M*.261.   (O.E. *wyrsa, wiersa.*)
pid, *sb.;* person, wight, *T*.592.   (O.E. *wiht.*)
pid, *prep.;* with, *T*.397, 398, etc.   (O.E. *pið.*)
pif, *sb.;* wife, *Jms*.265, 274; *M*.274; *T*.265, 274, 348, etc.; *piue, dat. s.,*
    T.424.   (O.E. *wīf.*)

wih-vten, see *piþ-uten.*

pile, *sb.;* while, time, *T.*514. (O.E. *hwīl.*)

pile, see *pille, vb.*

pilis, *sb.;* wiles, *T.*608. (O.E. *wīl.*)

pille, *sb.;* will, *M.*144, 234, 501; *T.*402, 430, 520, etc.; *wulle, M.*134. (O.E. *willa.*)

pille, *pr. 1 s.;* will, *T.*190; *pile, T.*535; *pille, pr. s., T.*355, 432; *pile, Jms.* 418; *T.*525, 606; *pele, T.*418; *pelle, T.*590; *pole, T.*623, 624, etc.; *T.*662 (desires evil counsel for thee); *wule, M.*118. (O.E. *willan.*)

pimman, *sb.;* woman, *Jms.*337; *M.*293, 337; *pimmon, T.*427; *vimmon, T.*442. (O.E. *wīfmann, wimman.*)

pin drunken, *adj. s.;* drunk with wine, *M.*282. (O.E. *wīn druncen.*)

winnen, *vb. inf.;* win, *M.*130. (O.E. *winnan.*)

wirche, *pr. subj. s.;* may work, *M.*134. (O.E. *wyrcan.*)

pis, *adj. s.;* wise, *W.*8; *Jms.*8, 65*, etc.; *Sp.*65*; *pise, W.*21; *Jms.*21; *T.*454. (O.E. *wīs.*)

pisdom, *sb.;* wisdom, *Jms.*96; *M.*96, 193, 247; *pisdome, T.*192. (O.E. *wīs-dōm.*)

pise, *sb.;* condition, *M.*113, 208, 209. (O.E. *wīse.*)

pisen, *vb. inf.;* teach, *W.*29; *Jms.*29. (O.E. *wissian.*)

pisest, *adj. supl.;* wisest, *W.*23; *piseste, Jms.*23. (O.E. *wisest.*)

pisliche, *adj. pl.;* wise, *W.*30; *Jms.*30. (O.E. *wīslīc.*)

piste, *pt. s.;* knew, *M.*309. (O.E. *witan.*)

pit, *sb.;* wight, person, *M.*237. See *pid.* (O.E. *wiht.*)

pit, *sb.;* wit, *M.*197; *T.*192; *pittes, Jms.*66. (O.E. *wit, witt.*)

piten, *vb. inf.;* know, *M.*221. (O.E. *witan.*)

piterliche, *adv.;* truly, certainly, *T.*660. (O.E. *witodlīce.*)

piþ, *prep.;* from, with, *M.*220, 249. (O.E. *wið*).

piþ-helden, *vb. inf.;* withhold, *M.*296. (O.E. *healdan* with prefix *wið.*)

piþ-innen, *adv.;* within, *Jms.*336; *M.*336; *piþ-innin,* inwardly, in secret, *T.*616. (O.E. *wiðinnan.*)

piþ-uten, *adv.;* outwardly, *T.*615; *prep.,* without, *Jms.*96; *wih-vten, M.*96. (O.E. *wiðūtan.*)

piue, see *pif.*

piued, *pr. s.;* wiveth, marries, *T.*277. (O.E. *wīfian.*)

wiuen, see *wyuen.*

pld, for *wilt, pr. 2 s.;* wilt, *T.*640, 649. (O.E. *wilt.*)

plite, *sb.;* face, beauty, *Jms.*266; *T.*266, 539. (O.E. *wlite.*)

wlonc, *adj. s.;* proud, *M.*141, 344. (O.E. *wlonc, wlanc.*)

po, *sb.;* woe, *Jms.*274; *M.*274; *T.*274. (O.E. *wā.*)

poc, *adj. s.;* weak, *T*.540; *poke, adj. pl.* as *sb., T*.554. (O.E. *wāc*.)

pod, *adj. s.;* mad, angered, *M*.281, 298; *pode, adj.* as *sb., T*.607. (O.E. *wōd*.)

poke, see *poc.*

polde, *pt. s.;* would, wished, would like, *W*.29; *Jms*.29; *M*.116, 218, 295; *T*.644; *pt. 2 pl., W*.27; *Jms*.27. (O.E. *willan, pt. s. wolde*.)

poldest, see *pelden.*

pole, see *pille, vb.*

ponin, *vb. inf.;* dwell, reside, *T*.642; *ponit, pr. s., T*.512. (O.E. *wunian*.)

pord, *sb.;* word, speech, *W*.21; *M*.311; *T*.424, 568; *pordes, gen. s., Jms*.361; *T*.361; *porde, dat. s., Jms*.21; *M*.287; *T*.591; *pordes, pl., T*.426; *pord, T*.453, 454. (O.E. *word, pl. word*.)

pord, for *porð, adj. s.;* worthy, *T*.643. (O.E. *weorþ*.)

pord-pod, *adj. s.;* word-mad, *M*.293. (O.E. *wōd* combined with *word*.)

porþe, pel porþe, *pr. subj. s.;* well be it for, *T*.592. (O.E. *weorþan*.)

pose, *indef. pro.;* whoso, whosoever, *T*.358. (O.E. *hwā swā*.)

pot, *pr. s.;* knows, *M*.169, 308. (O.E. *witan, pr. s. wāt*.)

poxen, *pp.;* grown, *M*.229; *poxsen, M*.161. (O.E. *weaxan, pp. weaxen*.)

prake, *sb.;* harm, *T*.606. (O.E. *wracu*.)

prakesih, *sb.;* peril, *M*.120. (O.E. *wræc-sīð*.)

praþþed, *pp.;* angered, *M*.288. (O.E. *(ge)wrāðian*.)

preche-dome, *sb.;* wretchedness, *T*.664. (O.E. *wræc* plus *dom.* Cf. *wræc-hwīl, wræc-sīð*.)

prench, *sb.;* trick, false idea, *M*.156; *prenches, pl., T*.388. (O.E. *wrenc*.)

writes, *sb.;* writings, *Sp*.66. (O.E. *writ*.)

pronke, *adj. pl.* as *sb.;* wrongs, *T*.555. (O.E. *wrang*.)

proþe, *adj. pl.;* angered, *M*.307. (O.E. *wrāþ*.)

pude, *dat. s.;* wood, *M*.162. (O.E. *wudu, dat. s. wuda*.)

puel, see *pel.*

puidepis, *gen. s.;* widow's, *T*.552. (O.E. *wuduwe, widuwe*.)

wule, see *pille, vb.*

wulle, see *pille, sb.*

purchen, *vb. inf.;* work, perform, *T*.396, 430; *purcheþ, pr. s.,* behaves, *M*.253; *purche, pr. subj. 2 s., T*.519. (O.E. *wyrcan*.)

wurhere, *adj. comp.;* of more worth, *M*.105. (O.E. *weorþra*.)

purmes, *sb.;* worms, *M*.504. (O.E. *wyrm*.)

purt, *sb.;* wort, herb, *M*.161. (O.E. *wyrt*.)

purþ, *adj. s.;* worth, *Jms*.105. (O.E. *weorþe*.)

wurthen, *vb. inf.;* worship, honor, favor, *Sp*.60; *purþen, T*.525. (O.E. *weorþian*.)

wurþen, *vb. inf.;* be, become, come, happen, *M*.141, 178, 232; *T*.359, 504; *þurden*, *Jms*.359; *purþen*, *pr. 2 pl.*, *M*.307; *purþe*, *pr. subj. s.*, let be, let happen, *M*.500, 501; *þur-þu*, *imp. s.*, be thou, become thou, *M*.281, 298. (O.E. *weorþan*.)

þurðscipe, *sb.;* honor, *Jms*.32; wurthecipe, *Sp*.32. (O.E. *weorðscipe*.)

wyuen, for ȝyuen (ȝiuen), *vb. inf.;* give, *M*.112; *wiuen*, *M*.117. (O.E. *giefan, gyfan*.)

ycnoþed, *pr. pl.;* know, *T*.631. (O.E. *gecnāwan*.)

yuel, *adj. s.;* evil, *T*.434. (O.E. *yfel*.)

ypille, *sb.;* desire, *T*.458. (O.E. *gewil*.)

7, symbol of *conj.* and.

BIBLIOGRAPHY

BIBLIOGRAPHY

Manuscripts and Editions

For detailed description of manuscripts and editions of *The Proverbs of Alfred*, see Chapter I.

Historical Material

A. Records

Birch, Walter de Gray. *Cartularium Saxonicum.* London: Whiting and Co., Ltd. (vols. I and II); Charles J. Clark (vol. III), 1885, 1887, 1893.

Kemble, John M. *Codex Diplomaticus Aevi Saxonici.* London: S. & J. Bentley, Wilson and Fley, 1839–48. Six volumes.

Domesday Book. Edited for the Record Commission by Abraham Farley (vols. I and II, 1783) and Henry Ellis (vols. III and IV, 1816), London.

Ancient Charters Prior to 1200. Edited by John Horace Round for the Pipe Roll Society. London: Wyman and Sons, Ltd., 1888.

Catalogue of Ancient Deeds. Prepared under the superintendence of the Deputy Keeper of the Records. London: Eyre and Spottiswoode (vol. I, 1890; II, 1894; III, 1900) and Mackie and Co., Ltd. (IV, 1902; V, 1906).

Pipe Rolls.

Roll of 31 Henry I. Ed. Joseph Hunter. London: no publisher, 1833.

Rolls of 2, 3, 4, Henry II. Ed. Joseph Hunter. London: Eyre and Spottiswoode, 1844.

Pipe Roll Series. Edited for the Pipe Roll Society. Rolls for 1158–78, 1180–88. London: Wyman and Sons, and other publishers, 1884–1925.

New Series of Pipe Rolls.

Rolls for 1190–94. Ed. Doris M. Stenton. London: J. W. Ruddock and Sons, 1925–28.

Roll for 1230. Ed. Chalfant Robinson. Princeton: The University Press, 1927.

Red Book of the Exchequer. Ed. Hubert Hall. *Rolls Series.* London: Eyre and Spottiswoode, 1896. Three volumes.

Liberate Rolls. For the reign of John. Ed. Thomas Duffus Hardy. London: Eyre and Spottiswoode, 1844.

Patent Rolls.

Rolls for 1201–1216. Ed. Thomas Duffus Hardy. London: no publisher, 1835.

Rolls for 1216–25 and 1225–32. Edited under the superintendence of the Deputy Keeper of the Records. London: Mackie and Co., Ltd., 1901, 1903. Two volumes.

Calendar of Patent Rolls. Edited under the superintendence of the Deputy Keeper of the Records. London:

Rolls for 1232–58. Mackie and Co., Ltd., 1906–8.

Rolls for 1258–72. Hereford Times Co., Ltd., 1910–13.

Close Rolls

Rolls for 1204–27. Ed. Thomas Duffus Hardy. London: no publisher (vol. I), 1833; Eyre and Spottiswoode (vol. II), 1844.

Series. Edited under the superintendence of the Deputy Keeper of the Records. Rolls for 1227–53. London: Eyre and Spottiswoode, and other publishers, 1902–27.

Feet of Fines.

Fines for 1182–97. Edited for the Pipe Roll Society. London: Wyman and Sons, 1894–96.

Fines for 1195–1214. Edited by Joseph Hunter for the Commissioners of Public Records of the Kingdom. London, 1835.

Rolls of the King's Court in the Reign of King Richard I (1194–95). Edited by Frederick W. Maitland for the Pipe Roll Society. London: Wyman and Sons, Ltd., 1891.

Dugdale, William. *Monasticon Anglicanum.* Edited with additional material by John Caley, Henry Ellis, and Bulkeley Bandinel. London: Longman (and associated booksellers), 1817–30. Six volumes.

Dugdale, William. *The Baronage of England.* London: T. Newcomb, 1675–76. Two volumes.

The Cartulary of Eynsham Abbey. Edited by H. E. Salter for the Oxford Historical Society. Oxford: Clarendon Press, 1907–8. Two volumes.

Sussex Archæological Collections. London: Published for the Sussex Archæological Society by John Russell Smith. Vol. I, 1848; XII, 1860.

Sussex Record Society Publications. London:

Vols. II and VII, *Sussex Fines.* Ed. L. F. Salzmann, 1903 and 1908.

Vols. VIII and XI, *Bishop Robert Rede's Register.* Ed. Cecil Deedes, 1908 and 1910.

Vol. X, *Sussex Subsidies.* Ed. William Hudson, 1910.

Vol. XXIX, *Abstracts of Sussex Deeds and Documents.* Ed. W. Budgen, 1924.

(All these volumes were published for the Society by Mitchell, Hughes, and Clarke, except II, which was published at Lewes by Farncombe and Co.)

B. Chronicles

Annales Monastici. II (Winchester). Ed. Henry Richards Luard. *Rolls Series.* London: Longman, etc., 1865.

Chronicon Monasterii de Abingdon. Ed. Joseph Stevenson. *Rolls Series.* London: Longman, etc., 1858. Two volumes.

Earle, John, and Plummer, Charles, (eds.). *Two Saxon Chronicles.* Oxford: Clarendon Press, 1892, 1899. Two volumes.

Florence of Worcester. *Chronicon ex Chronicis; Monumenta Historica Britannica.* Edited by Henry Petrie, assisted by John Sharp. London: Eyre and Spottiswoode, 1848.

Gaimar, Geoffrey. *L'Estorie des Engles.* Ed. Thomas Duffus Hardy and Charles Trice Martin. *Rolls Series.* London: Eyre and Spottiswoode, 1888–9. Two volumes.

Henry of Huntingdon. *Historia Anglorum.* Ed. Thomas Arnold. *Rolls Series.* London: Longman and Co., Trübner and Co., 1879.

Ingram, James. *The Anglo-Saxon Chronicle* (translation). London: J. M. Dent and Sons; New York: E. P. Dutton and Co., 1912.

Liber Monasterii de Hyda. Ed. Edward Edwards. *Rolls Series.* London: Longmans, etc., 1866.

Robert of Gloucester. *Metrical Chronicle.* Ed. W. A. Wright. *Rolls Series.* London: Eyre and Spottiswoode, 1887. Two volumes.

Simeon of Durham. *Historia Regum Anglorum.* Ed. Thomas Arnold. *Rolls Series.* London: Longmans and Co.; Trübner and Co., 1885.

Stevenson, William Henry (ed.). *Asser's Life of King Alfred.* Oxford: Clarendon Press, 1904.

Twysden, Roger. *Historiae Anglicanae Scriptores X.* London: J. Flesher and C. Bee, 1652.

William of Malmesbury. *Gesta Regum Anglorum.* Ed. William Stubbs. *Rolls Series.* London: Eyre and Spottiswoode, 1887, 1889. Two volumes.

DISCUSSIONS

A. General

The Introductions to the editions of the *Proverbs* by Skeat, Borgström, Hall, and Brown. See Chapter I, *supra*.

Middle English Texts used for comparison, etc. See footnotes, *passim*.

Atkins, J. W. H. "Early Transition English." *The Cambridge History of English Literature*, I, chapter XI. Ed. A. W. Ward and A. R. Waller. New York and London: G. P. Putnam's Sons, 1907. *The Owl and the Nightingale*. Cambridge: The University Press, 1922.

ten Brink, Bernard. *Geschichte der Englischen Litteratur*, I. Berlin: Robert Oppenheim, 1877. *Early English Literature*, I. Translation of the *Geschichte* by Horace M. Kennedy. New York: Henry Holt, 1883.

Gadow, Wilhelm. "Das Mittelenglische Streitgedicht, *Eule und Nachtigall*." *Palæstra*, LXV (1909), 1 ff.

Hinckley, Henry B. "The Date of *The Owl and the Nightingale*." *Mod. Phil.*, XVII (1919), 247. "The Date, Author, and Sources of *The Owl and the Nightingale*." *P.M.L.A.*, XLIV (1929), 329.

Skeat, Walter W. *Early English Proverbs*. Oxford: Clarendon Press, 1910.

Wülcker, Richard. "Über die Neu-Angelsächsischen Sprüche des Königs Ælfred." Paul and Braune's *Beiträge*, I (1874), 240.

B. Historical

Conybeare, Edward. *Alfred in the Chroniclers*. London: Elliot Stock, 1900.

Doubleday, H. Arthur, and Page, William (general editors). *The Victoria History of the Counties of England*. *Berkshire*. Ed. P. H. Ditchfield and W. Page. London: Vols. I and II, Constable and Co., Ltd., 1906, 1907. Vols. III and IV, St. Catherine Press, 1923, 1924. *Bedfordshire*. Vol. I edited by Doubleday and Page. Vols. II and III, by Page. London: Constable and Co., Ltd., 1904–8–12. *Oxfordshire*. Vol. II edited by Page. London: Constable and Co., Ltd., 1907. *Sussex*. Vols. I and II edited by Page. London: Constable and Co., Ltd., 1905, 1907.

Giles, J. A. *Memorials of King Alfred.* London: John Russell Smith, 1863.

Hearne, Thomas. *Spelman's Life of Alfred the Great.* Oxford: Printed at the Theater, 1709.

Lees, Beatrice A. *Alfred the Great.* New York and London: G. P. Putnam's Sons, 1915.

Mawer, A., and Stenton, F. M. *English Place-name Society Publications.*
Vol. I, Part 1, *Introduction to the Survey of English Place-names.*
Vol. I, Part 2, *Chief Elements in English Place-names.*
Vol. II, *The Place-names of Buckinghamshire.*
Vol. III, *The Place-names of Bedfordshire and Huntingdonshire.*
Vols. VI, VII, *The Place-names of Sussex.*
Cambridge: The University Press, 1924–30.

Simcox, W. H. "Alfred's Year of Battles." *Eng. Hist. Rev.,* (1886), p. 218.

"The Berkshire Downs." *The Saturday Review* (London), July 26, 1873.

"Two More Days on the Berkshire Downs." *Ibid.,* July 25, 1874.

Skeat, Walter W. *The Place-names of Berkshire.* Oxford: Clarendon Press, 1911.

C. Linguistic

Emerson, Oliver Farrar. *A Brief History of the English Language.* New York and London: Macmillan, 1896.

Gropp, E. *The Proverbs of Alfred.* (Dissertation), Halle, 1879.

Jordan, Richard. *Handbuch der Mittelenglischen Grammatik.* Heidelberg: Carl Winter, 1925.

Luick, Karl. *Historische Grammatik der Englischen Sprache* (Vol. I in six sections). Leipzig: C. H. Tauchnitz, 1914–21.

Morsbach, Lorenz. *Mittelenglische Grammatik.* Halle: Max Niemeyer, 1896.

Serjeantson, Mary S. *Distribution of Dialect Characters in Middle English.* Amsterdam: Swets and Zeitlinger, 1924.

"The Development of Old English ēag, ēah, in Middle English." *Journal of Eng. and Ger. Phil.,* XXVI (1927), 198 ff. and 350 ff.

Skeat, Walter W. *"The Proverbs of Alfred."* *Trans. of the Phil. Soc.,* 1895–98, pp. 399–418.

Wright, Joseph and Elizabeth Mary. *An Elementary Middle English Grammar.* Oxford: The University Press, 1923.

Wyld, Henry Cecil. *A History of Modern Colloquial English.* New York: E. P. Dutton and Co., 1920.

The Historical Study of the Mother Tongue. New York: E. P. Dutton and Co., 1906.

D. Metrical

Luick, Karl. "Geschichte der Heimischen Versarten." Paul's *Grundriss der Germanischen Philologie,* 2 Ed., II, Part 2 (1905), pp. 141–180. Strassburg: Karl J. Trübner.

Saintsbury, George. *History of English Prosody.* London: Macmillan and Co., Ltd., 1906–8–10. Three volumes.

Schipper, Jakob. *Englische Metrik.* Bonn: Emil Strauss, 1881, 1888. Two volumes.

History of English Versification (translation of an abridged version of the above, with additions and corrections by the author). Oxford: Clarendon Press, 1910.